John Lees is SSM Associate Priest in East Devon and Bishop's Officer for Diocese of Exeter. He has served for parish priest and also designing and He has advised the Church of Engl.  istry in secular employment. He was previously Assistant Diocesan Director of Ordinands for the Diocese of Chester and a pastoral tutor on the Northern Ordination Course.

His day job is working as a career coach. He is the author of 12 books on work and careers, including *How to Get a Job You Love* and *Secrets of Resilient People*. His books have been translated into Arabic, Georgian, Polish, Japanese and Spanish. He regularly contributes to *Harvard Business Review* online and in 2012 wrote the introduction to the *HBR Guide to Getting the Right Job*. He appears frequently in the national press and media. He works with a wide range of organizations on career issues and has delivered career workshops in Australia, Germany, Ireland, New Zealand, Mauritius, South Africa, Switzerland and several parts of the USA. He is the former Chief Executive of the Institute of Employment Consultants (now the Recruitment and Employment Confederation).

John is a graduate of the universities of Cambridge, London and Liverpool, a fellow of the National Institute for Career Education and Counselling and was a founding board director of the Career Development Institute. He is married to the poet and children's writer Jan Dean.

SELF-SUPPORTING MINISTRY:

A Practical Guide

JOHN LEES

First published in Great Britain in 2018

Society for Promoting Christian Knowledge
36 Causton Street
London SW1P 4ST
www.spck.org.uk

British Library Cataloguing-in-Publication Data
A catalogue record for this book is available from the British Library

ISBN 978–0–281–07845–5
eBook ISBN 978–0–281–07846–2

Typeset by Manila Typesetting Company
First printed in Great Britain by Ashford Colour Press
Subsequently digitally reprinted in Great Britain

eBook by Manila Typesetting Company

Produced on paper from sustainable forests

This book is dedicated to two places as
without them this book wouldn't have been written.
The first is Holyford Mission Community in
East Devon (incorporating churches in Branscombe,
Colyton, Colyford, Musbury and Southleigh). This is
where I currently serve, feeling hugely supported – especially
by the Rector, Hilary Dawson, who is an imaginative
leader and a great encourager of SSM. I am deeply grateful
to Hilary for providing a thorough review of this
book before it reached its final stage.
The second special place is Wilmslow parish
in Cheshire, which welcomed me as an SSM curate and
nurtured me for ten years. I consider myself extremely
fortunate to have had Tony Sparham as a
training incumbent as he firmly encouraged a
ministry focused on the world of work.

Contents

Acknowledgements

First, I would like to thank my wife Jan for the idea of writing this book.

The project would never have been completed without the generous advice and assistance of a wide range of people. My thanks go to Phil Aspinall and Jenny Gage for their comments on early drafts. I'd also like to thank all those who have shaped my thinking about SSM over the years: Loveday Alexander, Christine Bull, Hilary Dawson, Amanda Fairclough, Nick Fisher, Anne Futcher, David Herbert, Morwenna Ludlow, Kim Mathers, Ian McIntosh, Teresa Morgan, Sarah Mullally, David Nixon, Ray Samuels, Philip Sourbut, Becky Totterdell, Peter Shepherd, Christopher Southgate, Charles Sutton, Magdalen Smith, Paul Smith, Mike Williams and Roger Yates.

I'm indebted to everyone who kindly agreed to be case studies for this book (and also contributed all kinds of ideas and questions): Rob Fox, Jenny Gage, Biddi Kings, Mike Kirby, Jonathan Poston, Gina Radford, Tony Redman, Nick Shutt, Margaret Trivasse, Hugh Valentine and Gillian White.

The views expressed here are my own, and so are any mistakes.

1

Are you a vicar or what?

I am a self-supporting minister within the Church of England. It's a title I am relatively comfortable with and certainly better than many of the labels previously attached to unpaid clergy. Yes, in everyday conversation it would be much easier for me to have a simple title like 'vicar' or 'chaplain'; however, I recognize that many of my stipendiary colleagues have equally opaque job titles. Unpacking what we do, opening the door to the holy mysteries of church bureaucracy, is always an important chance to communicate.

My day job is working as a career coach, working with adults who want to make a career change or make the best of difficult work situations. Sometimes this is resilience coaching, supporting people through stressful episodes. I work with a range of organizations and people, including clergy. I'm the author of several books about work and careers – helping people who only meet me in print. I write and broadcast about careers issues in a range of media. This work is very much part of my calling, so I consider myself to be a 'minister in secular employment' (MSE – more on this later).

I am licensed to my local Anglican Mission Community – four parishes and five churches working together, served by one full-time (very proficient) rector. I'm part of a ministry team covering a wide range of services, events and pastoral needs. Flexibility in my work commitments allows me to assist in a number of ways and, in addition, I have a diocesan role as Bishop's Officer for Self-supporting Ministry, also performed on an unpaid basis. This balance of paid work, parish and wider commitments is fairly typical for a self-supporting minister (I'll use 'SSM' from here onwards).

Why this book, now?

Around four decades ago there was a flurry of writing about non-stipendiary clergy and worker priests. In 1983 the General Synod published Mark Hodge's *Non-stipendiary Ministry in the Church of*

England. Hodge observed that the growth of non-stipendiary ministry had occurred with 'very limited central direction and consensus' and argued for more of each. He argued that unpaid clergy had been ordained to enable mission but, in practice, they were generally allocated to local parishes and not offered further opportunities or development. Hodge was concerned to find 'a widespread view among stipendiaries that NSMs were an inferior class of clergy, not to be trusted in positions of responsibility or leadership' (Morgan, 2011, p. 5).

The seminal book *Tentmaking: Perspectives on self-supporting ministry* by James Francis and Leslie Francis provided a comprehensive overview. Many of the questions asked are still highly relevant to today's Church, but it was published in 1998 and much of its content came from previous decades (the most recent case study is dated 1991). A few shorter documents have dealt with SSM in the intervening years, but no book has taken the place of *Tentmaking*. A number of research studies have appeared, most notably the 2010 survey of SSMs in England, Wales and Scotland by Teresa Morgan. This book builds on this important study; I am grateful to the Revd Dr Morgan for her permission to quote several passages from her 2011 report.

What's happened since *Tentmaking*? Many things, of course, but the main one is a shift of focus. Twenty years ago the main discussion was about worker priests, MSEs and 'bridge' ministry. We now talk mainly about non-stipendiaries (known in Church of England circles as SSMs). The focus has shifted away from interactions outside church to the support SSMs give to parochial ministry. The term 'MSE' is heard far less frequently than it was 30 years ago – Chapter 8 offers an explanation.

Who might be interested?

All books about ministry are bound to fall into the expectation gap. For some, there will be too little focus on the bigger picture, the theology of ministry, the *why* rather than the *what*. This book touches on some theology, because all doing requires thinking. I will also review the history of SSM, because knowing how we got here tells us where we might go next. For some readers this may be less relevant than the nuts and bolts of ministry, especially working agreements and relationships.

This book is intended to be a practical guide to advise and support SSMs. This includes prospective SSMs as, although the role is fairly well understood by clergy, it's often a closed book to those considering a vocation to ministry.

I hope this book will inform those who select and train SSMs, and encourage those who work alongside them. It will perhaps assist diocesan leadership teams currently thinking about clergy selection, development and deployment. It focuses on the Church of England but should be relevant to unpaid clergy in other denominations. Therefore this book is written for serving SSMs, but may also be of interest to:

- individuals exploring SSM ministry as a vocation;
- diocesan directors of ordinands, bishops' advisers, and others involved in clergy selection;
- directors of ministry development and others responsible for ministerial training and development;
- ordinands in training and theological educators;
- stipendiary clergy who find themselves working alongside or responsible for SSMs;
- bishops' officers and advisers for SSM;
- senior clergy responsible for clergy deployment;
- congregations and teams working alongside SSMs.

Defining SSM

'Statistics for mission 2012: Ministry' defines 'self-supporting clergy' as ministers 'who do not receive a stipend'.[1] SSMs are mostly priests, although some are deacons. Readers and other lay ministers, retired clergy, and clergy in 'house for duty' posts are not considered to be SSM. A small number of unpaid clergy not yet retired operate on a permission to officiate (PTO) basis, but SSMs are nearly always licensed by a diocesan bishop. This process attaches the SSM to a specific benefice, where they are formally responsible to the incumbent (usually the working relationship is collegiate rather than supervisory). Most SSMs therefore work in a parish setting, with many also in paid employment elsewhere.

SSMs often dislike the term 'non-stipendiary' because this defines them in terms of financial status. Many people give their time freely to their church, including PCC members, church-wardens, Readers and other LLMs. Retired clergy offer substantial amounts of work, usually well into retirement. Stipendiary clergy also give some of their time freely for community commitments outside their job descriptions. Lack of pay is not the defining or most important aspect of SSM ministry – fulfilling the role of curate, priest or distinctive deacon, is what matters – taking care of people, being prophets, pastors and teachers, bringing people to faith, sharing their knowledge of God's loving presence, baptizing, blessing, absolving, and presiding at God's table. This is what calls and sustains SSMs, not role titles.

SSMs support themselves because they can, and because their contribution makes a difference. How do they support themselves? Some are retired and living on a pension provided by their employers (although as early retirement on a well-funded pension scheme becomes rarer, this will no doubt impact SSM availability). Others are semi-retired with enough financial independence to work almost full time in parishes. Many SSMs are in paid work – full time, part time or freelance. These SSMs inevitably have less time for parish work, but in fact still contribute many hours. Some consciously exercise a 'bridge' ministry between church and the workplace.

The Church of England pays for SSMs' training, but does not pay them an income while they train as curates. Neither the diocese nor the parish has to pay for SSMs' stipends, housing or pension contributions (this last element is very significant in terms of the number of clergy shortly to retire). All SSMs may claim expenses of ministry. Funds may be available from time to time to pay for, or subsidize, learning events and study. In some dioceses SSMs can claim part of the fee for funerals and weddings or make a claim for loss of earnings, although this is rare. However, as this book will later discuss, boundaries are shifting – some SSMs are being paid nominal fees for occasional offices, and some are working on a part-SSM and part-stipendiary basis.

At the time of publication there were 3,230 SSMs in England. SSMs form an increasingly large proportion of the clergy workforce – about a third of licensed ministers working in parishes. In some dioceses (Oxford and Bristol, for example) the ratio is higher. Teresa Morgan notes, 'In 60% of dioceses . . . SSMs form what we might regard as a typical 25–40% of clergy' (2011, p. 21). She also says:

> This figure is expected to increase in the next ten years, as around 40% of stipendiary clergy currently in post retire. The role that SSMs can and should play in the Church in the short and medium term is therefore a matter of obvious interest. The way they are deployed is certain to affect significantly the ways in which we can sustain and develop our corporate ministry and mission in the years to come.
>
> (Morgan, 2011, p. 4)

SSMs, along with stipendiary clergy, are subject to Common Tenure – documented terms of service linked to working agreements (see Chapter 9). They are accountable and subject to review processes including ministry development review (MDR).

The category SSM usually includes ordained local ministers (OLMs). Some dioceses continue to ordain OLMs. The idea is a positive one – encouraging communities to identify their own ministers. Other dioceses have never made sense of the theology of a geographically constrained priesthood. In practice, OLMs are often invited to operate outside their original parish limit, suggesting to many that the practicality (if not the theology) of OLMs might need to be reviewed. Most OLMs would consider themselves to be SSMs, although some feel that they are not given the same degree of recognition.

What do SSMs do?

When I explain my ministry to people who don't attend church, the question most frequently asked is, 'Do you do funerals?' The answer is 'Yes', of course, which people seem to find reassuring. Something about being engaged, literally, in life and death matters unlocks pastoral conversations. Many SSMs report similar conversations – which then usually move on to explain SSM, and how you can be ordained by the Church but not work for it. The first step is to explain that not all clergy are vicars. A former DDO colleague used to say, 'Priest is who you are, vicar/chaplain/associate priest/curate is what you do.' He'd often add a work role title when talking about MSEs: 'Priest is who you are, pharmacist is what you do.'

One assumption sometimes made is that SSMs perform a narrower range of duties than paid clergy. For example, it may be assumed that they don't preside at communion or they don't do weddings or funerals. So, to be clear, SSMs perform all the same rites as other clergy. SSMs might be called out at 2 a.m. because someone is dying, and they may take midweek communions. They will not have the same availability as full-time paid clergy, and probably won't routinely chair PCC meetings, but they are called (and trained) to do everything their stipendiary colleagues do. To date there has been one important exception – leading a parish. The Church of England has until now looked for a special set of abilities for clergy seen as potential incumbents. This book will explore why this thinking may be under review as SSMs are being used more flexibly and given more responsibility.

Most SSMs operate largely within the parish where they are licensed. This is not always where they live: 'Although the stereotype of SSMs is that they minister in their home parish, many, in practice, live some distance from where they are licensed' (Morgan, 2011, p. 17).

SSMs make an important contribution, especially to those many parts of the Church where shortages of clergy exist, or multi-parish benefices that require extensive travel and careful rota juggling. Their levels of responsibility vary; they may provide cover where an incumbent is on holiday or on sabbatical, and usually have increased responsibilities during a vacancy (but not always – see Chapter 11). The time commitment of SSMs varies, as does their focus of ministry. They tend to offer more hours than retired clergy. SSMs, like other clergy, take on community roles such as being school governors. Some SSMs serve as diocesan officers and advisers – for example, in vocations work or advising on spirituality. Most bishop's officers and advisers for SSM are unpaid.

Some SSMs (perhaps describing themselves as MSEs) have a special relationship to their 'nine to five' working lives. They are licensed to parishes, but see their paid work as their primary calling (see Chapter 8). Other SSMs have a ministry focused on community. Training clergy whose focus of ministry is outside the Church is still Church of England policy, but some argue that in its efforts towards maintenance it is leaning too heavily on a middle-aged workforce of 'free' clergy, neglecting callings to other contexts. Teresa Morgan points to a key finding of the 2010 survey:

> One of the most surprising and, to the designers, saddening results of the survey was how few respondents saw themselves as having much, if any ministry outside the formal structures of the Church. This has some claim to be one of the survey's most significant findings, and one which, if it prompts a response, has the potential to make a substantial difference to the future of the Church . . . It is a great pity that more SSMs do not think of their ministry as extending beyond the formal bounds of the Church. It is also a sad omission that the Church does not encourage them.
>
> (Morgan, 2011, pp. 19–20)

A changing picture

Today many English dioceses are planning increased dependency on SSMs. This is largely for two reasons. The first is a projected decline in church attendance and income. The second is the fact that even if funds are forthcoming there will be fewer stipendiary clergy available. Since a considerable proportion of clergy are over 50, many will be retired by 2025. Dioceses are thinking hard about how they can continue to support worshipping communities with dwindling resources; some are taking a strategic view about SSM deployment. One or two are wondering if more SSMs might be found, and thinking about how to get more out of their existing SSMs. Some SSMs report that they are being asked to take on an increasingly large workload to support a shrinking workforce of stipendiary clergy.

Other SSMs are being used more imaginatively than they have been previously, being given levels of responsibility that would have been unusual 20 years ago. In the recent past it was considered unthinkable for SSMs to have charge of a benefice. This was already changing in 2010: 'Some, but not all, dioceses currently allow SSMs to look after a parish within a group' (Morgan, 2011, p. 14). In fact, as Chapter 4 demonstrates, SSMs are now working as unpaid incumbents. There is reason to assume that SSMs will be invited to undertake interim ministry. They continue to work in diocesan officer roles. Their role in vacancies may also change – consideration is being given to providing short-term licences to SSMs during extended vacancies.

This reinvention of SSM is energizing and positive. To date it has been largely ad hoc, local and without a great deal of national attention or policy-making. SSMs come with valuable skills and experience. This is sometimes fully recognized, but not always. They are sometimes overworked, sometimes sidelined, sometimes frustrated. The good news is that evidence is emerging, if slowly, that they are being deployed with more creativity and being considered more strategically as a resource for ministry.

Case studies

This book is intended to be about ministry in practice, so it will come as no surprise that it includes a range of case studies – examples of the different ways in which SSMs work. The variety of their ministry is enormous, and I could quite easily have put in four times as many case studies without repeating stories. I have, however, tried to cover a range of ministries, experience levels and locations. Many dioceses also publish very useful case studies of their own SSMs.

SSM in practice

Tony Redman, SSM, St Edmundsbury and Ipswich Diocese, chartered building surveyor

How and why I became an SSM

I was licensed as a Reader in 1976. I didn't feel called to serve as a local non-stipendiary minister (LNSM), probably because of the geographical limitations imposed. Some years later I was offered a range of roles, including the job of diocesan surveyor. I felt called to ordained ministry at the same time, but chose to join an architectural partnership. I've served as an SSM in Suffolk for about 14 years.

My experience of SSM

I think we put ministers in silos too early, and this includes Readers. Strict demarcation lines really don't reflect the reality on the ground of holding things together, particularly in a rural context. We look after four parish churches and we have two OLMs, two Readers, three elders, one stipendiary priest and myself. Our experience is that we need to get people to contribute according to their skill, not their status. Elsewhere I've seen examples of high-value SSMs not being used adequately and sad evidence of transferable skills in SSMs being ignored or wasted.

What's the main focus of my ministry?

Having worked full time for many years in an architectural practice, I now work one day a week as a consultant building surveyor, and otherwise most of my time is taken up in ministry, including the work I do as Bishop's Adviser for SSMs. Apart from my parish responsibilities, which take at least 15 hours a week, I volunteer as a chaplain at my local hospice.

Support and training

I was ordained in 2003 having been trained on the East Anglia Ministerial Training Scheme, where I undertook a Master's in pastoral theology. I found this invigorating and challenging – I'm still building on the work I did in my Master's degree, especially in relation to change management.

I'm not sure how much the course prepared me for life as an SSM, but I was at least encouraged to think about the contribution I could make as a priest in secular employment. However, I have reservations about the way courses don't really fit us for the practicalities of ministry, relying too much on curacy training. My training was delivered largely by stipendiary priests and theologians, who had sympathy with but little understanding of SSM. In general, ministerial training doesn't address workplace ministry – you have to work it out for yourself.

Challenges and difficulties

I think that the Church does not adequately prepare ministers, stipendiary or otherwise, for the challenges of working with a multidisciplinary team of colleagues, including volunteers. We need to seriously rethink the idea that some people are exercising ministry in their 'spare time', and learn from organizations that have been using volunteers at a professional level for many decades – the National Trust, for example.

I think the primary challenges for SSMs are inevitably about status. I firmly believe that we should work to people's gifts and not their status, but the Church doesn't always agree. Also there are very evident work pressures on many SSMs: most of the time, working agreements seem to be fictional! At one stage I couldn't work out how you could be a priest *and* have a family *and* an outside job, but we work it out in the end. Largely this is about having really clear boundaries focused on a minister's well-being.

I'm also concerned about the lack of national representation of SSMs, especially on the General Synod. SSMs make a very significant contribution to church life, and this really isn't represented in terms of national discussions.

The best thing about SSM

The strongest aspect of SSM, for me, is *diversity of presence*. In a rural context you still need to be a kind of Herbertian embedded presence and, even as an SSM, demonstrate visible leadership. I very much enjoy flexibility in my ministry, but I also enjoy working in a professional context, particularly where I can raise an awareness in fellow clergy of the theology of the buildings we use, and their potential for ministry.

Looking forward

Since becoming Bishop's Adviser for SSMs, I like to encourage fellow SSMs to talk positively about their experiences, using Luke 10 as a focus. When I was thinking about SSM, I could not see how the various pressures on life could be balanced with serving as a member of the clergy, and so I try and encourage SSMs to be open with others about their personal experiences of how they manage the work/life balance.

SSMs often, like me, value flexibility, but we also need to retain a sense of *discipleship*. We have to take the rough with the smooth, doing what's required and not reinforcing the stereotype that SSMs pick and choose. In fact, I think it's like being a chameleon, fitting into the context and not just in what you are comfortable with. I've considered full-time ministry but I'm not tempted by it – for me, SSM ticks all the boxes.

2

A question of identity

This chapter explores the nature of SSM in more depth, looking at why SSMs are needed and what happens when their role is misunderstood.

SSM – the right language?

Unpaid clergy feature in all parts of the Anglican Communion and have been part of the Church of England since the early 1960s. Various titles have appeared: 'auxiliary pastoral ministry', 'auxiliary parochial ministry', 'part-time ministry', 'supporting ministry', 'honorary ministry' and 'non-stipendiary ministry' (NSM). During the last decade 'self-supporting minister' has become standard. According to Teresa Morgan's 2010 survey, '46% of respondents to the survey preferred to be called SSMs; 23% preferred NSM, while 23% called themselves OLMs' (Morgan, 2011, p. 1). 'NSM' is still in use in some dioceses and other parts of Anglican Communion, but 'SSM' now holds sway. Margaret Whipp (in Witcombe, 2012, p. 15) suggests that 'SSM' is still problematic: 'arguably it draws undue attention to the financial security and largesse of the minister'. Role titles are slippery.

Obstacles to recognition

Without dwelling on negative issues, it's worth rehearsing some of the misunderstandings and prejudices encountered by SSMs. They're voiced by a wide range of people: a training incumbent, a churchwarden trying to negotiate clergy availability, a rural dean organizing chapter events, senior clergy planning for deployment, a bishop welcoming an experienced SSM into a new diocese. SSMs still hear references to 'second-class training' (not always in hushed tones). SSMs can find that both their congregations and the wider community are mystified by their role, and they face the same repeated questions:

'You're a lay priest, right?'
'It must be hard being a curate for ever.'
'Are you still in training?'
'Are you a chaplain?'
'When are you going to have your own parish?'

The last question seems the most common; people assume that SSM is a passing condition. Morgan explores these questions with a firm corrective:

> Almost all SSMs are used to hearing themselves denigrated as hobby priests, weekenders or volunteers. (To describe unpaid clergy as volunteers or hobbyists is not only condescending but theologically indefensible. All clergy are called to their vocation. No ordained person is a volunteer.)
>
> (Morgan, 2011, pp. 13–14)

Terms like 'hobby priest' are insulting, just as similar language would be to auxiliary firefighters, volunteer coastguard officers, special constables or reservists in our armed forces. Even though some of these roles receive financial compensation, the analogy is important. There are many contexts where unpaid professionals work alongside salaried colleagues, enabling organizations to provide a more flexible service. Sometimes, their contribution makes the difference between stretched provision and no provision at all. My grandfather, a blacksmith in a busy shipping port, also served as an auxiliary railway fireman. No one asked him why he did it or whether he had divided loyalties.

As SSMs become an increasingly familiar feature, the picture is changing. Negative assumptions have not disappeared, but they are less frequent – and more often challenged. Even so, SSM awareness is not universal. SSMs arriving in a new parish cannot always be confident that a congregation will understand their function. Colleagues may assume they are not available for most activities, and therefore omit them from meetings or rotas out of misplaced kindness.

Why SSMs?

As Chapter 3 will explore, the idea of SSM has gained traction for multiple reasons. Although it was expedient to appoint clergy not requiring a stipend or pension, the main benefit imagined was attracting individuals whose working experience would enrich the Church. The first reason was utilitarian, the second idealized. The two motivations coexist today and, arguably, the first has more weight, with the result that SSMs are still usually seen as support for the incumbent. Rod Hacking's picture in 1990 is still familiar today:

> With regard to the development of non-stipendiary ministry the essential change allowing men and women to be ordained while continuing in their secular occupations has taken place. There is however considerable resistance to this being anything other than some kind of 'back-up' to the existing form and shape of the Church, in which NSMs can even be seen as an answer to the problem of shortage of clergy and money.
>
> (Hacking, 1990, p. 23)

Robin Greenwood, in *Transforming Priesthood*, argues:

> there remains . . . a disproportionate emphasis on the role of the clergy to the detriment of the whole body of the church. With unexpectedly glorious exceptions, it is still the case that the majority of parishes regard the presence of a priest, preferably male and stipendiary, to be the major requirement and resource for the church to flourish and engage in its work.
>
> (Greenwood, 1994, p. 50)

Called to SSM

Society wants and needs clergy. Every month the media carries articles along the lines of 'my struggling local parish' or 'six churches with just one unpaid vicar'. Even so, we remember that SSM is about responding to a calling, not just to a need. Not *calling to*, which often feels too role-specific, but calling *by* and calling *for*. We are all (depending on your theological limits, 'all' might mean 'congregations', 'baptized Christians', the 'people of God' or even 'all') called to respond to God's gifts and God's presence. We are called to hear and retell some of the most important stories shared by humanity, and as a result required to shape our lives in a faith-driven direction. We are called to minister to each other, but (partly by listening carefully to the experiences of the first Christian communities) to appoint individuals who can do 'God stuff' in an organized way. This is what organized ministry is about – setting aside people to do things that make a difference. In church language, this means individuals who can bless, absolve and invite to God's table. In everyday language, there is work to be done teaching, caring, building community, gathering, praying and being alongside people at the most difficult and joyful moments of life. But there are wider conversations – opening eyes to God's presence, helping people to make sense of their lives. There is a prophetic element, too – recalling people to truth and hope.

SSM is not just a functional convenience. It is not second prize, but a distinct calling. Some of the most important outward-facing ministries are exercised by SSMs, whose work is the connective tissue that binds today's Church to working families, as well as to the vast range of institutions, employers, professional bodies and communities that have no natural point of engagement with organized religion. Faith is relational, so needs to be interested in all kinds of relationships and connections.

Where SSM works well, it is supportive but also subversive. That's not about being 'difficult' (SSMs have no special prerogative here). Being subversive is, of course, a gospel imperative – to question tired assumptions and speak truth to power. SSM is necessarily and healthily subversive where it operates outside the Church's normal sphere of influence, because that's where many interesting people and conversations are found. SSMs, by being placed in at least two worlds simultaneously, find themselves questioning and redefining what church is for. This is 'radical' in the deepest sense of the word – connecting to our roots; one of the rewards of SSM is being in the right place to ask the right questions.

The problem with inherited structures is that they have inherited thought patterns attached, resistant to scrutiny because they are woven into tradition. Radical alternatives are by no means new.

Dietrich Bonhoeffer, for example, questioned the professionalization of the clergy:

> The church is church only when it is there for others. As a first step it must give away all its property to those in need. The clergy must live solely on the freewill offerings of the congregations and perhaps be engaged in some secular vocation. The church must participate in the worldly tasks of life in the community – not dominating but helping and serving.
>
> (Bonhoeffer, 2015, p. 486)

The first SSM ordinations in the 1960s offered a quiet revolution, suggesting that bigger changes to patterns of ministry were on their way. However, the mould has not been broken, but reshaped. After all, the model of vicar and parish is long established. The stipendiary model will continue to be important, offering stability and continuity. Valuing SSM must not in any sense mean devaluing the vital work done by stipendiary clergy.

SSM is not just one thing, and it is not what it was. There are signs that the proportion of licensed clergy who are SSMs is increasing (although much depends on how many SSMs are ordained and how many retire). SSM is being rethought at the chalkface as the need for associate leadership develops. To date the Church's selection processes have largely assumed that two kinds of clergy were being ordained: paid incumbents with measurable leadership potential and unpaid assistant ministers unlikely to hold a leadership role. This binary thinking is under scrutiny because it doesn't reflect what's happening on the ground – especially where the traditional model of 'one priest in one church' is impossible.

Unpaid professionals

The term 'professional' has a range of meanings. Traditionally, professions required a high standard of education, which in general meant that they were only open to those with means. More recently the term has described work where high standards are maintained: decorators and gardeners are just as likely as solicitors or architects to use the word 'professional' in describing their services.

Using the term 'professional' in relation to unpaid workers is rarer and slightly more problematic. Professionals have always performed some unpaid work – lawyers working on a pro bono basis, for example, or doctors working for international charities. Reservists apply their skills within the armed forces for part of the year (paid an allowance plus a bounty, but not on the main pay scales). Skilled professionals often work free of charge as charity trustees, coastguards, archaeologists, counsellors, adult literacy tutors, mentors, conservation workers, sports coaches and fundraisers.

Should SSMs be treated differently?

Increasingly, dioceses are giving more attention to their SSMs. As they grow in impact and in number, it makes sense to think about how they can be supported. Morgan argues that it is a tribute to the Church of England that SSM exists at all:

> so many non-stipendiaries are in service, wanting nothing more than to use their time, energy and talents to further every aspect of our shared life and mission. The need now is for a strategy to use them better, to enable the Church to fulfil more of its mission more effectively in the years ahead.
>
> (Morgan, 2011, p. 29)

There is much to be done, some of it very straightforward. A minority of dioceses currently say something about SSM on their websites. Many (but not all) dioceses have a bishop's adviser to look after and represent SSMs. The most common reason stated for lack of SSM officers is superficially positive: 'we treat all licensed clergy the same'. In practice this can mean that dioceses do not respond to SSMs as well as they could. Treating SSMs 'equally' can sometimes lead to not considering them at all. In contrast, most dioceses have a senior staff member, often a dean on the bishop's staff, to represent ordained women. There are different groups of ministers, and some groups have distinctive development needs. Furthermore, where an organization deploys both paid and unpaid professionals there will clearly be a need for different HR strategies in terms of working arrangements, expectations, development needs and accountability. Providing for the particular needs of certain kinds of clergy is not about treating people as separate or different, but about tailored support.

Recognition and growth

The case studies in this book outline the experiences of a range of SSMs. In an online article Rodney Schofield asked, 'How serious is the Church of England about its non-stipendiary ministers?' He offered a fairly negative overview:

> They have been welcome as makeshift priests to help out during interregna, and to cover holidays and times of illness, but otherwise they have been invisible in the normal deanery and diocesan structures. Chapter meetings, for example, frequently take place without them, and when pastoral committees assess 'ministerial needs and resources' the underlying assumption often seems to be that the system hinges on the deployment of stipendiary priests. NSMs have been seen as assistants who relieve something of the pressure on the full-time clergy, but who cannot – because of their freedom of mobility – in the last resort wholly be relied upon.[1]

Teresa Morgan's report points to similar tensions existing in 2010:

> 'I do feel that paid clergy do not take SSMs seriously,' comments one respondent, 'and view us as amateurs not to be trusted.' 'Since moving from stipendiary to nonstipendiary,' says another, 'I have become aware of the disdain with which some stipendiary clergy view SSMs.' Several have been asked, 'Are you a proper priest or an NSM?'
>
> (Morgan, 2011, pp. 13–14)

In the book *Diverse Gifts*, MSE Sara Scott argues: 'Non-stipendiary ministry ought not to be a cut-pricing way of staffing a parish but a distinctive ministry with its own characteristics . . . The ordination of men and women to be non-stipendiary priests presents an opportunity to the Church that has not yet been fully grasped' (Torry, 2006, pp. 57 and 63). Some argue that having decided that the main role of the SSM is to assist in the parish, little needs to be done after their licensing. Morgan points to concerns about SSM development:

> both anecdotal evidence and the results of this survey suggest that SSMs are not, in general, being actively developed or deployed by their dioceses, and in some cases are being actively hindered in their ministry. Many SSMs are aware of this and unhappy about it. Some have tackled the problem in their own ministry, but it seems clear that the Church as a whole would benefit from a strategy to use SSMs better.
>
> (Morgan, 2011, p. 5)

There are clearly issues, some fundamental, many of them obstacles to progress, frequently being aired but not always addressed. Surveys of SSMs legitimately point to frustrations and disappointments – but there is a positive dimension. It's important to remember that all clergy surveys point to frustrations, but for most clergy, paid or unpaid, ministry is fulfilling. A majority of SSMs surveyed in 2017 reported high levels of role satisfaction and a continuing sense of calling (Church of England Ministry Division, 2017, p. 4). This is mirrored in Teresa Morgan's research:

> It may sound from parts of this report as if the predominant tone of responses to the survey was grumpy. In fact, nothing could be further from the truth. The words which recurred most often in the final comment box were 'privilege' and 'joy'. One respondent speaks for many: 'I feel passionate about my ministry and how privileged I am to be able to draw alongside people and minister to them in a wide variety of contexts.' It was heartening to find that despite the difficulties many experience, nearly all respondents had a powerful sense that they were working out their vocation.
>
> (Morgan, 2011, p. 28)

The Church needs talented ministers, and it can't afford to pay for all of them. Yes, there are difficulties. *And yet* – and there's something in that phrase about the way good things happen in sometimes dysfunctional contexts – and yet . . . SSM can be responsive, grounded, connected, prophetic. It is undeniably life-changing. One of the profoundly important aspects of this ministry is that it provides opportunities for men and women to respond to God's call – in a way that would not be possible if only stipendiary clergy were ordained. An experienced MSE in London wrote about the way his hopes for ministry in secular employment were dashed continually against the rocks of institution. However, when asked the question, 'Would you do it all again?', his answer was unhesitating: 'In a heartbeat.'

SSM in practice

Jenny Gage, SSM, Ely Diocese, freelance maths educator

How and why I became an SSM

When I was ordained in 2010, I worked in higher education focusing on school mathematics education, having been a secondary school mathematics teacher. It was clear to me that stipendiary ministry wasn't going to be an option, not least because of family circumstances including my husband's work. I took early retirement in 2014 from full-time paid employment, but I still undertake freelance work as an educational consultant, and also do research as a practical theologian. I'm also a very committed granny!

Over time, I've come to realize that the call I have is to sit on all kinds of margins, and so my portfolio life suits me well. I guess I could have become a full-time SSM in parish ministry when I left paid employment, but in the five years between ordination and retirement, I came to realize that my call is not to traditional parish ministry, but to live out a call as a priest in different contexts, and also to research what that means.

Participants in my SSM research have found that some parish clergy don't really understand their vocation, asking why we need to be ordained at all, if we're going to continue in secular employment. For myself, I have a strong sense of coming full circle to something that was always there, and that a core part of my identity in God is as a priest in his Church, so my answer would be that it's not about what I needed or need, but about God's specific call to me.

My experience of SSM

I'm currently licensed as an associate minister to a group of four parishes in Ely Diocese. I am on the rota for worship three Sundays out of four, I take weddings and funerals, attend ministry team and PCC meetings, and assist with a variety of parish activities, according to how much time I have available.

I am also Bishop's Officer for Self-supporting Ministry in the Diocese of Ely, a role I find stimulating and enjoyable. There is an obvious pastoral aspect to the role, but I also have opportunities to represent SSM colleagues in diocesan planning, and to help SSM curates growing into their roles.

What's the main focus of my ministry?

As an SSM with a portfolio working life, I find it hard to identify one main focus of my ministry. Sometimes, my main focus will be the parish; at other times, it might be my freelance work or my research or my family. In these areas, I see my ministry worked out not only through pastoral contact with people, but through the way in which my work is part of realizing God's kingdom here on earth.

Support and training

I greatly enjoyed my training on a course, which helped me in my formation as a priest in secular employment. On the course, there was a small but useful nod towards MSE through a session in which a speaker from Christians in Secular Ministry (CHRISM; <www.chrism.org.uk>) helped us to think about what workplace ministry might look like.

My training as a curate involved attendance at evening events which sometimes felt like curtailed, tired versions of the training which had taken place during the day. It was pretty exhausting. We did have some training about associate ministry, including a helpful session on 'leading from the second chair'.

Challenges and difficulties

Dioceses need SSMs. About a third of licensed clergy are SSMs, but stipendiary ministry (SM) is still very much the 'default' mode. Where SSMs fit that mould, they are often taken for granted, and where SSMs don't fit the mould they are not always treated particularly well.

Another issue for me at the moment is the way we have lost sight of MSEs. In its vocational criteria, the Church assumes that MSEs can only be in place with the consent of their employer. In my experience employers are generally happy if one of their employees becomes an MSE but in today's culture of diversity they are unlikely to do more than that. That's a reality the Church needs to grasp quickly; we need to rethink any assumptions that clergy must have written agreements with employers like those they have with incumbents.

One of the biggest challenges SSMs experience is managing the expectations of colleagues and congregations. Managing your own expectations can be hard too – we all want to do everything perfectly.

The best thing about SSM

I've enjoyed the opportunity to undertake research among my SSM colleagues in secular employment both in Ely Diocese and elsewhere, and have had a lot of very useful conversations and experienced a high level of mutual support. That's important for SSMs, who can feel a little isolated. I think what we share is a growing sense of recognition and identity.

I think we also share a sense that some of us are called to the unique situations in which we find ourselves, and that God wants us to live our lives as priests in the world as well as in church and the parish.

Looking forward

I still feel I'm growing into the role, but that every part of me, all of who I am, is called to priestly ministry – including the things I do outside church.

3

A brief history

The fiftieth anniversary of the first ordinations of SSMs was marked in 2013. How did we get here? This chapter offers a brief history of self-supporting ministry.[1]

Bishop Russell Barry, in *The Relevance of the Church* (1935), made perhaps the first reference to 'non-stipendiary ministry', but the idea was much older. Rod Hacking writes: 'Non-stipendiary ministry was a long time coming. Or perhaps, we should say, it was a long time arriving, for it could be said that it was the original model for ministry, at least as far as the New Testament is concerned' (Hacking, 1990, p. 7). Paul was, of course, the first self-supporting minister. Paul learned from Gamaliel, who encouraged his students to practise a trade so they could support themselves. We know that Paul continued his work during his travels, making tents from animal skins. Although some argue he was only partially self-supporting, while exercising his ministry he must also have given quotations, raised bills and chased debts.

If self-supporting pastors have always existed, why is the Church attached to a stipendiary model? It has obvious benefits in terms of workforce planning, stability and continuity. The model also has strong New Testament roots: the disciples were inspired to walk away from their trades. Like Jesus, these early followers lived on the kindness of strangers. Some returned to fishing, briefly, until they met the risen Christ, understood the task ahead, and left their occupations for ever. This is the picture of ministry we are most familiar with – a single-focus activity not distracted by worldly concerns. Absolute commitment, it seems, requires turning away from all ties, including paid employment. So, if Paul as tentmaker offers one model, a second is a calling *away* from work. Arguably, neither model is presented as superior: 'it is clear from the New Testament that the exercise of ministry within the Church does not preclude the possibility that the Minister may engage in a secular occupation' (Hacking, 1990, p. 9).

Clergy having a secondary form of employment has always been a feature of church life. Even so, the Church of England demonstrated a historical resistance to unpaid clerics, for a range of reasons. Medieval abuses confused the idea of being self-supporting with being venal. Post-Reformation clergy in England were required to avoid impropriety, and were supported by a benefice – income from glebe lands and tithes – although historical documents illustrate that a 'living' was not always enough to live on. Farming, teaching and academic work were all considered suitable supporting occupations; most other forms of work were not. In 1972 a standardized stipend was introduced – not a salary, but a sum designed (alongside other benefits including housing and a pension) to protect clergy from the distractions of financial need.

Objections to clergy having separate paid work reflect the comfortable perspective of the developed world. Other parts of the globe know the self-supporting pastor well. A colleague visiting a Kenyan parish found that the local priest was most keen to show visitors his smallholding and animals. For many clergy around the world self-sufficiency is the norm. Bi-vocational ministry is in vogue in North America (see Chapter 11), where ministers are employed part time by the Church and expected to find additional paid work elsewhere.

Developments in the nineteenth and twentieth centuries

In the second half of the nineteenth century the Church of England considered ordaining working men as deacons. The 1859 Convocation of Canterbury dismissed the notion as 'threatening the status and admission requirements of the clerical profession' (Vaughan, 1987, p. 39). It was felt that clergy in alternative employment would undermine the idea that priestly ministry was a dedication to a single life purpose. There was (and still is) confusion about outcomes. Would the Church be ordaining clergy who had sufficient private means to work unpaid? Or clergy who would continue in their present occupations? Would 'volunteer clergy' simply support existing structures or add something new?

Innovation was, nevertheless, in the air. The Church of England continued to discuss proposals to ordain 'men who had other means of living' as deacons. The idea was put aside, but in 1866 the office of Reader was re-established. In 1878 the Lambeth Conference learned that a government doctor had been ordained deacon in Jamaica. In 1886 the Bishop of Manchester ordained the managing director of a cotton-spinning company, who went on to work with no official ecclesiastical office (Vaughan, 1987, pp. 39 and 56). One barrier to change was the 'professionalization' of the nineteenth-century clergy (see Percy, 2006). From a medieval distaste for wealthy clerics we move into a purist ideal – professionalism untainted by commerce. The 1887 Convocation of Canterbury felt that the idea of a man holding down two professions simultaneously was self-evidently contradictory. This was perhaps a blinkered view even for its time, given the number of amateur scientists and artists in the Victorian era.

In 1925 the Archbishops' Committee report objected to similar proposals – not just because of the alterations required to the Ordinal and canon law, but also the risk of 'occasions on which a man's professional duty would be in conflict with his duty as a priest'. Anthony Russell captured some of the flavour of this debate:

> no professional can view with equanimity the implication that its functions can be adequately performed either on a part-time basis or as a hobby . . . A man either is or is not a member of the profession. There is a sense in which the Augustinian and medieval doctrine of the indelibility of the priestly character is a theological statement of this aspect of a professional role, and in some form this doctrine is held by many clergy.
>
> (Russell, 1980, pp. 286–7)

Russell goes on to suggest that this new breed of unpaid clergy might be considered as 'sub-professions' (rather as legal executives are to lawyers and accounting technicians are to accountants). This is not how the role has developed.

Justin Lewis-Anthony notes the demise of the 'one church, one vicar' mode. Referring to the increased presence of retired and SSM clergy, he writes, 'If "The Village Pub" were to have an accurate sign, the village parson would need to be shown as retired, or working in another profession' (Lewis-Anthony, 2009, p. 25), reflecting a frequently voiced nostalgia for a time when every parish had a stipendiary priest in charge. Martyn Percy provides a different perspective, suggesting that ministry as a profession 'has never been something easily agreed upon. Neither, for that matter, has it ever been something the Church of England could easily afford . . . They want to be regarded as specialist purveyors of knowledge, rights and techniques – "technologists of the sanctuary"' (Percy, 2006, pp. 72–3).

Allen's 'voluntary clergy'

Nineteenth-century reformers pressed for a broadening of ordained ministry, often as a way of responding to changes in society. Thomas Arnold proposed a revival of the order of deacons, but the best-known proponent of 'volunteer clergy' was Roland Allen (1868–1947). Ordained in 1893, he served as a missionary in northern China. After returning to England in 1907 he resigned a parochial position in reaction to a debate about baptism policy, and spent the rest of his career as an unauthorized non-stipendiary. In his 1923 book *Voluntary Clergy*, Allen argued for self-sufficient congregations, far less dependent on a central institution. This work continues to be influential. Allen's view:

> The stipendiary system grew up in settled churches and is only suitable for some settled churches at some periods: for expansion, for the establishment of new churches, it is the greatest possible hindrance. It binds the church in chains and has compelled us to adopt practices which contradict the very idea of the Church.
> (Interview with Roland Allen, quoted in Stevens, 1985, p. 129)

Allen's proposals were frustrated by the Lambeth Conference of 1930, but in the same decade the first NSMs were ordained in Hong Kong. Interestingly, 'Within two decades 43 per cent of that diocese's clergy were in secular employment' (Fuller and Vaughan, 1986, p. 175). Arguments for change were pushed forward by others (notably Frank Russell Barry in his book *The Relevance of the Church*, published in 1935), but it took the social upheaval of the Second World War to clear the way for a new model, influenced by the French worker priest movement, described by David Edwards as the 'most courageous and extensive experiment undertaken by any Christian church anywhere to bridge the gulf fixed since the nineteenth century between organized religion and the working classes' (Edwards, 1961). In his book *Britain's First Worker-priests* John Mantle extensively documents how this movement developed:

Following the French, a small but dedicated group of mainly
Anglican clergy went to work in parts of industrial Britain . . .
showing that working life was their vocation too . . . in practice,
Britain's first worker-priests had much more in common
with their counterparts in France; they were theologically
well-educated and conventionally trained clergy, 'priests turned
workers', who had resolved, as a priestly vocation, to live and
work alongside their fellow men and women in manual labour.

> (Mantle, 2000, pp. xxi and 2–3)

This starting point was conceived as a way of reaching out to particular communities. It drew on the French worker priest model, but
with important differences, as Edward Wickham describes:

a different model was developed as more appropriate to the
British scene, the model of 'industrial mission' as it came to be
known in Sheffield after the war. Highly selected clergy at that
time were deployed to the larger industrial organisations and
a new style of ministry was pioneered. But it was still a professional ministry.

> (Francis and Francis, 1998, p. 205)

Writing in 1974, Wickham also noted that 'though the number of
clergy and ministers in secular jobs increases, few become genuine
worker-priests, manual workers, engineers and factory workers'.

The decline of the worker priest movement was in some ways
structurally dictated: 'Eventually, the institutional decision was
taken to set up Industrial Mission, and as a consequence the church
establishment failed to foster worker priests in England' (Fuller and
Vaughan, 1986, p. 178). John Mantle analyses why the English worker
priest movement came to an early end:

For generations the territorial parish had been viewed as the
only proper context for mission and ministry – the only way
of being the church – and the handful of worker-priests, and
some industrial chaplains who believed otherwise, were voices
crying in the wind. Rather, the institution, which implicitly
refused the worker-priests recognition, threw its weight behind
the burgeoning non-stipendiary ministries, especially where
these supported the parochial system, and where participants

remained in middle-class and professional occupations, occasionally appropriating the title 'worker-priest' or 'priest-worker' for themselves. And the same institution, for which a moment in that post-war world had appeared to sanction an engagement with industrial society by new and radical means, gradually abandoned even that, and returned to its true focus of concern: internal debates and the maintenance of the territorial parish.

(Mantle, 2000, p. 4)

Southwark and 1963

From the 1950s onwards amendments to canon law were proposed to remove restrictions on secular work (early proposals suggested that NSMs should be directly responsible to a bishop). By the Lambeth Conference of 1958 it was agreed that there were no theological obstacles to ordaining someone continuing in a lay occupation. The critical moment was when Mervyn Stockwood acted unilaterally by establishing the Southwark Ordination Course, ordaining the first six candidates in September 1963. In 1983 there were 15 courses offering part-time clergy training.

Initially there were restrictions on how such clergy might be used. It was felt that they should stay in the parishes where they were ordained, and would not be permitted to be incumbents – 'they can never operate independently of a beneficed clergyman' (Russell, 1980, p. 286). The view of SSMs had expanded by 1985, when General Synod outlined five different categories of NSM, one of which was work-focused ministry. Later measures looked extensively at selection and training.

Did we get the SSMs the Church originally had in mind?

The steps taken in 1963 were extraordinary – not just in reading the zeitgeist, but decisively cutting through a great deal of red tape. The impact was enormous, first because it authorized ordained ministers in the workplace in a new way (not as industrial chaplains, but as an ordained presence in places of work). Second, it enabled a whole new range of ministries within the Church.

A brief history

The 1963 Southwark ordinations offered an opportunity to rethink ordained ministry. The driver was not budgets, but the chance to draw on a new talent base – people who bridged work and church. Within a few years of this event Michael Ramsey wrote, in the first edition of *The Christian Priest Today*:

> I regard the contemporary development of a priesthood which combines a ministry of word and sacrament with employment in a secular profession not as a modern fad but as a recovery of something indubitably apostolic and primitive ... What we call our 'auxiliaries' today belong most truly to the apostolic foundation, and we may learn from them of that inner meaning of priesthood which we share with them.
>
> (Ramsey, 1972, p. 4)

The gap between this last sentence and current thinking is profound. Considering the reputation of *The Christian Priest Today* – 'as close to an expression of ministerial theology as the Church of England has' (Lewis-Anthony, 2009, p. 79) – it is interesting how little is written about this combination of ministry and paid work Ramsey celebrated as 'indubitably apostolic' and as a realization of the 'sacred within the secular'. For example, Rod Hacking's *On the Boundary*, published in 1990, contains the following in a foreword by George Carey:

> I don't need convincing of the value of the non-stipendiary minister. But while I'm committed to it, I am also very concerned that over the last 10 years or so it seems that we have lost our way a little. There was confusion about whether the ministry should be work-based or church-based, there has been some confusion about the identity of non-stipendiary ministry, leading to a steady trickle of people shifting into stipendiary ministry; there has been apathy on the part of some leaders, incumbents and lay people to affirm and support the ministry of the non-stipendiary disciple.
>
> (Hacking, 1990, p. vii)

This is not, of course, the only perspective. Anthony Russell outlines issues raised by the introduction of what he describes as 'Auxiliary Parochial Ministry':

> Some clergy believe that the Auxiliary Pastoral Ministry results from a mistaken theology of the priesthood; others that it

28

is misguided as a matter of policy; others that it is merely a response to inflation and its alleged biblical legitimation is merely making a virtue out of necessity. However, there are others who regard this new form as heralding a radical reshaping of the church's ministry which will eventually lead to its indigenization in working-class areas and its penetration of areas of society, particularly those concerned with work, from which the Church now realises itself to be alienated.

(Russell, 1980, pp. 286–7)

Russell's suggested 'reshaping' of ministry is evident, but it is harder to see how the 'auxiliary' clergy he describes have helped the Church speak into communities it was not reaching before 1963.

The Church of England was attracted to the idea of volunteer clergy initially for a variety of reasons, some idealist, some pragmatic. One was to build on a minister's secular work rather than seeing it as preparation for ministry. Another driver was to reach new communities. Owen Chadwick, instrumental in his 'Tentmakers' article in *Theology* in 1951, outlined four primary 'motives' for ordaining unpaid clergy (see Francis and Francis, 1998, pp. 81–2). I take the liberty of expanding on them as follows:

- **parochial** to respond to parish need, particularly in areas where clergy are in short supply;
- **economic** the financial burden of stipends and pensions;
- **evangelistic** the idea that 'worker priests' are able to open doors through access to different communities and by being able to speak their language (very much a response to the perceived class bias of the post-war Anglican Church);
- **industrial** a ministry presence in the workplace not confined to workplace chaplaincy (see Chapter 8).

Some argue that the Church has lost sight of the last two of Chadwick's objectives. Martyn Percy suggests that economic pressures continue to influence change more than theology:

Various categories of minister have sprung up in the gap created by the smaller numbers of paid priests in the Church of England, and also to reflect the ambivalent attitude that prevails in relation to ministerial provision . . . Schemes have ranged from a voluntary diaconate (first proposed in the mid-nineteenth century, but regularly resurrected as an idea) to Auxiliary Pastoral Ministry (APM), which was later to become known as Non-Stipendiary Ministry (NSM). Many dioceses now have Ordained Local Ministers (OLMs). In addition to these categories, the number of 'sector ministers' – chaplains in hospitals, the armed services, prisons and education – has risen significantly. The blurring of the boundaries between full-time and part-time ministry, and the emergence of 'house-for-duty' clergy, has also meant that there are difficulties in specifying what constitutes 'professional' ministry in the Church of England; it no longer means 'paid', if it ever once did.

(Percy, 2006, pp. 73–4)

Did the Church get the ministers it had in mind? MSEs are shrinking in number, largely because the Church is locked in uncertainty about how to authorize them. The pressures of parochial need increasingly take priority. Many SSMs have an important ministry at work, often unnoticed by the institution. In this respect, we still live with the confusions of identity outlined by Carey.

SSM today is also, however, varied, important and often leads to high levels of role satisfaction. We may not have the SSMs we originally had in mind, but we have made progress in many new ways. The fact that SSMs are integral to parish life in many parts of the UK argues that we have moved into very new thinking about calling, function and earning a living.

SSM in practice

Jonathan Poston, Rector of All Saints, Wingerworth, Derby Diocese, osteopath

How and why I became an SSM

When I originally trained on the Northern Ordination Course I was working full time as an osteopath in northern Manchester. I felt a strong calling not only to the Church but to my patients and to the local community. I served as a part-stipend, part-SSM curate in Manchester before moving to Derby Diocese.

My experience of SSM

As an SSM I wanted to keep a strong connection with people outside the Church, operating in the 'borderlands'. Even while I was in training, the fact that I had a ministry alongside my work as a qualified osteopath enabled all kinds of interesting conversations.

What's the main focus of my ministry?

Having served as an SSM for a number of years, I was attracted to my current role because I felt it was time to lead in a parish context. Since 2014 I've been looking after a parish on the edge of Chesterfield on a 0.5 basis. Although I am provided with a house, in practice I need to maintain income from osteopathy work in order to keep my head above water. This provides interesting pressures, because I work one day a week in Matlock and another day in Manchester. It's a struggle to find time for anything else but work – as is often the case for clergy in part-time roles, the job could easily take all hours available. And often feels like it does!

Support and training

I have concerns about the ever-increasing workload of clergy in general and the level of support which is available – to stipendiary, SSMs and clergy like me who are mixing both modes. Clergy seem less able to support each other as everyone is so busy and there seems to be a reluctance for the Church to invest financially in structures to support clergy. More and more is put on to clergy, which leaves little room for development or growth, particularly if you're working on a part-time basis.

Challenges and difficulties

I enjoyed working as an SSM in the 'borderlands', but it has its challenges. If you're the kind of person who can live in two worlds at the same time, that's great, but it can sometimes feel as if you are neither fish nor fowl. In a way, moving into a more conventional parish role is often the easiest course of action – perhaps that's why a number of SSMs switch to a stipendiary or house for duty role.

The best thing about SSM

In the past, where most of my working time was focused on osteopathy, I really enjoyed the opportunities for special kinds of conversations with my patients, and so the healing work I was doing was very much as an extension of ministry. It was also important to me to engage with the business community and representatives of other faiths. Working in a very different context these days I can say I enormously enjoy the challenges of being the rector of a thriving community, working with a positive and energized team who also understand the pressures I am under still having to work two days a week out of the parish.

Looking forward

There's lots to do and I'm looking forward to the years ahead.

4

At the turning point?

This chapter looks at how SSMs feature as part of the clergy workforce, the time they give to ministry, and their important roles connecting the church to the wider world.

The changing shape of ministry

The Church of England's ministry statistics relating to 2016 include the following information.

- The number of stipendiary parish clergy continues to decline. There were 9,509 in 2002, 8,120 in 2013, and in 2016 there were 7,788.
- There were 3,230 SSMs in 2016, down from a total of 3,300 in 2015. Previously the number of SSMs had been increasing; in 2002 there were 2,091.
- The number of ordained local ministers (OLMs) fell from 530 in 2012 to 450 in 2016.
- In 2015 and 2016 SSMs represented around 29 per cent of licensed parochial clergy, the highest proportion ever recorded.
- In the period 2012–16 the balance between SSM and SM ordinations has varied. In 2012 the balance was almost 50/50. In 2015 there were 315 SMs and 183 SSMs ordained. In 2016 the respective figures were 299 SMs and 185 SSMs.
- In 2016, 27.7 per cent of SMs were women (up from 26.9 per cent in 2015); 51 per cent of SSMs were women, the same proportion as 2015.

In 1901, there were around 25,000 parish clergy in England. In 2016 the total number of stipendiary clergy fell below 8,000 for the first time. The report 'Ministry statistics in focus: Stipendiary clergy projections 2015–2035' points to a 'steady decline in the total pool of diocesan stipendiary clergy if the current trends of ordinations and retirements continue' (Church of England Research and Statistics,

2016, p. 14). Including retired clergy, at a parish level there are two unpaid clergy for every stipendiary.

The proportion of clergy who are SSMs has been increasing, but held steady between 2015 and 2016. In some dioceses this figure has, anecdotally, reached 50 per cent. Some predict that within the next 20 years around 40 to 50 per cent of licensed clergy will be self-supporting. This projection is uncertain, since it is difficult to predict future numbers of SSMs being ordained and how many will retire or transfer to stipendiary posts.

Numbers are only part of the picture. Fewer stipendiary clergy are being ordained, and there is less money to pay for them. Even so, the lion's share of parish work, especially administration, is undertaken by stipendiary professionals. Active retired clergy assist in large numbers. There appears to be declining interest in house for duty positions (working part time in return for paid accommodation). Many dioceses are therefore rethinking deployment. Some parts of the Church are planning to work on a multi-benefice or mission community basis (see Chapter 11). Experimental models of collaboration are under discussion, oversight ministry being an important example, imagining a future where ministry teams (primarily lay) are supported by one or two ordained facilitators.

SSMs, as a third of the licensed workforce, are clearly making an important contribution in terms of hours and activities. In 1977, Robin Gill offered a theological reflection using the terminology of the time:

> It is necessary to give some clarity to the somewhat cumbersome term 'non-stipendiary ministry'. It refers, of course, to those priests or ministers, varied in their functions and training, who work for the churches whilst not actually receiving their main salary from them. That is not to say that they receive no payment or expenses . . . but that the churches are not the main providers. Whether because of outside employment or because of a pension from such employment, non-stipendiary ministers always have a greater degree of financial independence from the churches than their stipendiary counterparts.
>
> (Francis and Francis, 1998, pp. 267–8)

Gill was prescient in writing of 'their *main* salary'. One of the features of today's Church is the development of a mixed economy, blurring the lines between SM and SSM. For example, some clergy are working part SM and part SSM, required to find additional paid work while in a part-time clergy appointment. One case study in this book runs a mission community as an SSM rector; another works as a part SM, part SSM. Some dioceses pay SSMs part of the fee for conducting a funeral or wedding, others don't.

SSMs' hours given to ministry

The 2015 'Experiences of ministry' survey looked at the weekly hours worked by clergy. Stipendiary incumbents indicated an average of 50.2 hours. SSMs contribute on average around 30 hours of church work – 30.3 hours for SSMs, 31.6 hours for OLMs, plus a surprising 29.8 hours for MSEs. At 30 hours a week in broad terms, that's more than the median for part-time workers (16.2 hours in 2017, according to the Office for National Statistics) and fast approaching the ONS median of 37.5 hours for full-time work. With over 3,200 SSMs in English dioceses contributing something approaching 100,000 hours weekly, even using the national living wage as a benchmark, the costs saved run to tens of millions of pounds.

The point of this figure isn't to induce guilt among diocesan staff or to seek financial compensation for SSMs. It's important to be clear on this point. Most SSMs are entirely happy to work for nothing, and prefer to do so. Many take their expenses but put more in the collection plate. However, all work is contractual, even if no pay is involved. Generally, volunteers expect things in return, especially where they are working at a professional level. High on many ministers' lists are items such as support, encouragement and positive feedback. Sometimes this is very evident, but there are underlying patterns of neglect. SSMs are often required to take on extra workloads at times of change or difficulty (for example, in a vacancy or where a colleague is off sick). More than a few SSMs report a lack of support during such times.

Untapped potential?

Given that, in some dioceses, SSMs represent nearly half the licensed clergy, they have to date attracted little discussion. Recent publications have looked at resilience, emotional work and burnout in ministers, but these studies focus largely on stipendiary clergy. In recent decades considerable attention has been given to fresh expressions of ministry. Again, little of this thinking has explored the role of SSMs. Perhaps even more importantly, little has been published about how to make the best use of them in future. Sweeping and inaccurate assumptions are made about SSMs' potential, deployability and flexibility. One block to discussion is the view sometimes put forward that 'SSMs vary so much they're impossible to manage'. SSMs do indeed vary. SSMs in full-time work are often able to assist in parishes at weekends or in the evenings. Others are retired or semi-retired and have a great deal of time to offer. Some feel underused.

Too often, decision-making is based on the idea that SSMs are unreliable, inflexible and 'not deployable'. This is unimaginative and out of date. Teresa Morgan is not alone in arguing that the classification 'deployable/non-deployable' is increasingly inappropriate:

> The difficulty with SSMs is not that they are not deployable; it is that dioceses do not include them in their planning. If, as part of an overall strategy for clergy deployment, dioceses identified the places where non-stipendiary hours were most needed, they might find that SSMs were very willing to transfer their ministry there. If that happened, it would also create more opportunities for SSMs to develop their ministry. Dioceses would be making better use of their human resources, and deployability would not be an issue.
>
> (Morgan, 2011, pp. 16–17)

The Church needs new thinking to manage this complex volunteer workforce, looking at other organizations who manage unpaid professionals. The deployment of SSMs will no doubt require greater attention to the pressures they experience, and the strengths they bring to their roles. Although SSMs put in more hours than many part-time workers in other industries, evidence suggests that they are reasonably resistant to burnout. In the report 'A closer look at self-supporting and stipendiary ministers in the Experience of Ministry Survey 2013 dataset' (Clinton, 2014), one interesting finding was that 'SMs report greater emotional exhaustion than SSMs'. Further research might discover whether SSMs avoid damaging stress because of the nature of their roles or whether the balancing of life required by SSM naturally aids resilience.

Bridge building

SSM is without doubt a bridge ministry, connecting worshipping communities to society at large. Bridge ministry is about creating traffic – an exchange of ideas from opposing shores. This ministry is about listening and translating, bringing the concerns of work and community into church, allowing them to dwell in a quiet, reflective place. Theological connections are made, helping world and church to make sense of each other, understanding why people feel frightened and hopeless. Nearly all bridge ministry asks difficult questions, challenging inhuman decisions, especially when they are justified by empty platitudes. Prophetic ministry can involve challenges to language that has been emptied of meaning. For example, modern society co-opts terms such as 'calling' and 'passion' without considering the costs of commitment. Every organization seems eager to say something about its values without always considering how words translate into actions. In this context, the Christian message can be uncompromising in its clarity – examining issues through the lens of the Gospels, making sure the Gospels do not sound like arcane code, and then calling the world to its senses.

The 'circumstances of the life already being lived'

All Christians are called to live out discipleship in daily life, which for many includes work. In 1945, *Towards the Conversion of England* stated: 'We are convinced that England will never be converted until the laity use the opportunities for evangelism daily afforded by their various professions, crafts and occupations' (Press and Publications Board of the Church Assembly, 1945, p. 58). Work adds a great deal to life – intellectual stimulation, community, friendship, learning, meaning and self-esteem. It can also be a place of stress, anxiety and drudgery, and something we want to escape.

The 2017 report 'Setting God's people free' found that '59% of those of working age said that the most challenging context to be a disciple of Christ was the workplace' (Archbishops' Council, 2017). As with the 1997 report 'Is anybody listening?',[1] respondents felt they heard little in teaching and preaching that helped them in the place they spent most time – work. 'Setting God's people free' notes examples of workplace ministry. Its intention was to encourage lay leadership and participation, so it is perhaps not surprising that no mention was made of ordained ministers. Even so, this was perhaps a missed opportunity to revisit the potential of MSEs.

Some SSMs do not see their work as a place for ministry, but as a means of subsidizing time in the parish. These individuals are sometimes the most likely to switch to stipendiary status (sadly confirming the assumption that ministry inside church is the 'real deal'). Many others take the opposite view and see the workplace as central, often working as unlabelled MSEs. CPAS Resource Sheet 8, 'Non-stipendiary Ministry', realistically points out that:

> some MSEs . . . have no official status in the workplace. Nevertheless, because their fellow employees know that they are ordained, those in difficulties approach them for pastoral help and guidance. They may also be recognised by other Christians as a focal point and source of encouragement in Christian witness.[2]

MSEs, official or not, keep the Church informed about the world of work and offer distinctive support to congregation members coping with the pressures of employment. MSEs and worker priests provoke a deeper understanding about God's presence in all forms of human activity, as argued on the website 'With-Intent: Worker-priests and MSEs':

> The underlying theology of all manifestations of MSE/ worker-priest ministry is one of solidarity and identification. This is as irresistibly clear and powerful a purpose to those called to it as it is incomprehensible or merely weird to those who are not. It is quite different to models of chaplaincy . . . It seeks to overcome the separation that exists between 'the church' (conceived of as the institution) and the world of work. It seeks to serve the church – as institution and more importantly as the wider, mystical body of Christ.[3]

Being church at work

Even before the worker priest movement, some English clergy undertook paid work outside the Church, not as a means of subsistence but in order to embed themselves in their communities. In 1994 Robin

Greenwood argued, 'The everyday ministry of laity at work and in the community goes largely unsupported' (Greenwood, 1994, p. 171). This statement seems as true today as it was four decades ago. There are few current examples of authorized, ordained workplace chaplaincy. The fact that it was also known as 'industrial chaplaincy' offers one explanation – it was a movement intended to reach working-class communities in the 1950s, reliant on mining, heavy industry and manufacturing. These sectors still exist, but changed almost beyond recognition. In 1945, a quarter of a million operatives worked in deep coal mining; the last deep mine in the UK closed in 2015.

SSMs who wish to exercise an informal workplace ministry feel particularly unsupported and isolated at present, something reinforced when ministry development reviews neglect to ask the question, 'Tell me about your ministry outside the Church.' This question should be mandatory for SSMs.

I personally conducted a piece of informal research in 2017, looking at the workplace ministry of recently ordained SSMs. Many described a strong calling to be ordained and remain in work. None felt their ministry is formally recognized – some were unsure if they were entitled to call themselves MSEs (see Chapter 8). It was clear, however, that their presence and ministry is appreciated by work colleagues. While the Church is slow to recognize this ministry, it seems that employers are comfortable doing so. Some related warm, open conversations with senior management about the extent and nature of their ministry. Direct evangelism seems to be rare and often inappropriate; more commonly, pastoral contact leads to occasional offices and the beginnings of faith journeys. Most frequently the experience (as described by one respondent) feels like 'getting on with the job and doing it as well as you can while working alongside and supporting other people'.

At present the Church appears to lack the capacity to engage with those parts of SSMs' ministry that are offered outside the parish. If workplace ministry is largely unacknowledged by the institution, other ministries are also invisible. Teresa Morgan summarizes the situation:

> few respondents saw themselves as having much, if any ministry outside the formal structures of the Church . . . Those who did report ministering outside church did so in many different

ways, including at work, through personal contacts and social networks, via the internet, by serving on committees, and through volunteering. Their ministry was equally varied, from sharing the gospel in groups or one-to-one, to praying with and for others, formal or informal counselling or taking regular and occasional offices. MSEs, in particular, see every part of their lives and work as witnessing to the gospel. This list gives just a taste of the great opportunity which is currently being almost entirely missed by the Church. Most SSMs spend much or most of their time outside formal church structures. They are, together with lay people, the natural missionaries to our society. They have far greater opportunities than most stipendiary clergy for spreading the gospel in the secular world.

The Church, however, does almost nothing to prepare SSMs and lay people for this ministry, to support and encourage them in it, or to provide resources for their development.

(Morgan, 2011, pp. 19–20)

The idea of *ministering by working alongside* draws on powerful theology. Affirming work is a way of affirming God's universal presence, but it's also arguably an underappreciated way of helping people make connections between everyday experience and faith. Work is a place of choices, ethical dilemmas and personal growth, and (as many clergy acknowledge) a great deal more can be done to make sense of work in faith terms. The idea (explored further in Chapter 6) that God is found and shared in the ordinary stuff of life has strong New Testament roots. There is something incarnational and generous, too, in an understanding that God works *in* and *through* situations and people, not around them.

For the Church of England, is this a turning point in ministry? Looking at SSMs in numerical terms, the jury is out. However, it's clear that as resources are spread more thinly, we need to maintain a steady focus on what church is for. The debate isn't just about maintenance and growth, it's about rediscovering the impulse to reach those outside the four walls of church. It isn't only about engagement in the workplace, but potentially about reconnecting with what *The Invisible Church* describes as 'churchless Christians' (Aisthorpe, 2016) – people who believe themselves to be Christian but no longer belong to a church community. And so, we return to the fact that

SSMs are called to a place where they are needed – not just in terms of parochial duties, but reaching the whole people of God. Rod Hacking writes:

> A faith in a living God who is not limited to the boundaries of religion, a recognition that the Church is nothing more than a means to an end, and the call to become more human – the three represent the heart of what any prospective ordinand requires. To these, for an NSM, must be added a willingness to live it out within the particular circumstances of the life already being lived. It is not about going somewhere else to find security in a role and a structure that caters to your needs, but being and serving where you are now. It is not easy – but for the sake of the Kingdom of God, it is there on the boundary that they are called to be.
>
> (Hacking, 1990, p. 149)

SSM in practice

Nick Shutt, SSM Rector, West Dartmoor Mission Community, Exeter Diocese, retired solicitor

How and why I became an SSM

I worked for a number of years as a solicitor and continued to do so after I was ordained as an SSM in 1994. I enjoyed the challenge of exercising a bridge ministry between church and world, but also found it difficult to provide everything the church needed. Hours were long as church time was fitted in after a full day in the office and took up most weekends. The overlap was in some way strong for me because I have a LLM degree in ecclesiastical law from Cardiff University, which means that I have been able to combine my interests in both law and ministry. Parochial ministry certainly has plenty of opportunity to use legal expertise.

My experience of SSM

I retired after 25 years of being a solicitor to take on the role of rector of this busy mission community which brings six parishes together. It's a matter of principle for me that I do this on an SSM basis – the role needs to be filled and I don't need a stipend. Working as an SSM also gives me, I believe, better insights into the ways to get the most out of teams of volunteers. I know what it is like to have to turn out for a church meeting at the end of a busy day in the office.

What's the main focus of my ministry?

I serve as SSM rector, looking after six parishes in the West Dartmoor Mission Community. At present I believe I'm the only SSM in charge of a mission community in this diocese, but there have certainly been SSMs running parishes. Rather bizarrely, there are two stipendiary colleagues who are part of the team here as well as Readers and retired colleagues. This is a role I have fulfilled now for nine years.

Support and training

How well was I prepared for what I'm doing now? Reflecting back on the support I received during ordination training and my curacy, I'd have to say that I can't recall very much focus on what ordained ministry might be like for somebody working full time. In practice, it can be extremely difficult to fit in all the learning requirements of the course. Training events for curates often tend to exclude people who are working full time.

Challenges and difficulties

One of practical disadvantages of SSM is that because there is no stipend income received, it is not possible to offset any working expenses for income tax purposes. In contrast, SMs employ specialist tax consultants to make the most of concessions available to clergy who receive a stipend; these are not available to SSMs. Everything is paid out of taxed income with no deductions possible.

It has been my experience that SSMs are also discriminated against by organizations when it comes to applying for grants. The Ecclesiastical Insurance Group will not entertain grant applications from SSMs, for example. A sabbatical taken after 20 years of ministry was entirely self-funded, whereas an SM colleague received a £500 grant towards his sabbatical from the diocese. It was all I could do to beg £45 for a train fare to London.

Fulfilling the role of SSM rector has highlighted many challenges that often are not seen by those fulfilling more conventional SSM roles. The sheer weight of ecclesiastical bureaucracy which goes with multi-parish ministry is the most obvious example.

The best thing about SSM

SSM makes you visible in the local community, who soon come to know you are 'good for nothing'. The ambiguity of this phrase echoes the ambiguity of the way in which SSM is seen, both within and outside the Church. It spawns many questions that give opportunities for meaningful conversations. There is a different dynamic when you do something as a volunteer as opposed to being a 'paid-up member' of the organization that is the Church. People recognize it. It certainly gives a sense of freedom and, while I take the oath of canonical obedience seriously, there is a freedom in being able to think, 'What are they going to do, sack me?' What could be better than journeying with people and sharing Christ because it is something I love doing – it is my calling.

Looking forward

I recognize that I'm now in an unusual position as an SSM working as a full-time rector, but I'm guessing that many people across the country will be doing what I'm doing within a few years.

5

Called to the margins

This chapter reflects on what it means to be called, in words often used by SSMs, to a ministry 'on the edge'. For example, Gill Mack, contributing to *Tentmaking* about her work as a deacon and midwife, writes:

> Ministry in secular employment must be free from much of the structure of parish and ecclesiastical life but *not* totally free. The Minister in secular employment is the fool on the edge of both worlds who must retain, at all costs, the freedom to cross the boundaries and often to live in the no-man's land in between.
>
> (Francis and Francis, 1998, p. 326)

Edges have two characteristics – distance from the centre and closeness to other objects. SSMs sometimes feel as if what they do is peripheral and half-visible. Sometimes their ministry feels disconnected from the 'main event' of church life. At other times they feel their deepest calling is expressed in some of the most important places.

Called to a context or a way of life?

The word 'religion' was traditionally understood to have its origins in 'discipline', 'rule' or 'duty' – sometimes linked to the idea of liturgy as the 'work' of the faithful. An alternative reading (Lewis-Anthony, 2009, p. 148) sees connections to the word 'binding' – not in the sense of coercive control, but in the way ligaments bind the human skeleton. Religion potentially binds people together in healthy working structures. This reinforces the well-known idea that religious activity is about *belonging* as much as *believing* – shaping a community of faith.

This idea is relevant here; SSM is a calling to a context and a community. For the ordained local minister this context, at the point of ordination at least, is obvious. However, for SSMs the context may be broader. SSMs often live outside the parishes they serve and sometimes have strong community connections independent of the Church. Here they can reach parts of society where church has little contact. That good soundbite, 'The Church is the only institution that exists primarily for the benefit of those who are not its members', is attributed to William Temple. SSMs are, like chaplains, clergy who are a gift to non-members. They provide the only contact many people have with Christianity, beyond the occasional funeral. Here is a distinctive reversal of the norm: only SSMs can be an ordained presence in this space.

An uncertain calling?

Any discussion of what shapes ministry is inevitably a discussion about calling. My work in the careers field makes me aware of the way individuals normally make decisions about their future. The process used by the Church of England to select ordinands offers several parallels – but also significant differences. Some of my colleagues in the careers field express considerable interest in this discernment process. Allowing time for calling to be explored so thoroughly is deeply counter-cultural in an age when we expect quick decisions and instant feedback. Slowing things down, allowing a calling to articulate itself and commitment to a long-term role – these are rare and valuable. Most people spend only a few hours a year making career decisions (it's claimed that we spend more time planning a holiday than thinking about career choice). Employer selection processes normally take a few weeks; in contrast, those offering themselves for ministry begin a process that will take at least a year of discussions, new experiences and reflection. The Church's tradition of discernment comes from generations of good practice based on patience, faith development, encouragement and the gradual unfolding of vocation.

Although the Church of England's selection process is imperfect (like all methods), it has much to commend it. In contrast to a world where people are expected to be self-directed individualists, the process is rooted in community. Candidates are put forward by communities and their calling needs to be evident to them. The process is more about 'us' than 'me'. Selection by the Church of England involves triangulation – the individual must show that they feel called, certainly, but their calling must also be seen by others (not just the congregation). Finally, calling needs to be identifiably useful. That's why the Church looks for candidates whose vocation is clear, realistic and informed. A calling is clearly from God, but in selection terms it also needs to be *to* something – a context.

I make this point to remind myself that discernment and calling are the beginnings of the process that shapes SSMs. Remembering the primacy of calling is important. It reminds us that callings are equal and so are all ordinations. It reminds us that SSMs are often called to be an ordained presence where they are – sometimes more than a parish role.

Calling and compromise

How and why are people called to SSM? For some, SSM seems an appropriate 'fit'. Some don't feel called specifically to SSM; it's where the church places (or pushes) them if they don't look like potential incumbents (see Chapter 11). Some candidates feel they have little choice – family or work commitments can make it difficult if not impossible to consider full-time training. Even committing to a vocations process can provide significant pressures, so SSMs need to think clearly about the compromises they will face in training and ministry. Sometimes other time or geographical constraints get in the way as well.

These are genuine issues; the problem is that they can be experienced as forms of failure – 'I'd like to be a full-time vicar, but . . .'. SSM candidates often sound apologetic and it's easy to see why. Nearly every learning event SSMs go through, from the moment they enter the selection process onwards, has a single focus: parish ministry. This agenda drives curate training, most chapter meetings, most diocesan courses and ministry review. There are, arguably, pragmatic reasons for this, as there is much work to be done with and for congregations – but it is not the only work and not where most people are.

There is therefore a strong implicit bias towards one shape of ministry. We need to be more honest about naming this unspoken bias. Through training and into ministry, by the questions they are asked and the opportunities presented, SSMs repeatedly feel they are judged by the amount of time they give to a parish and viewed as subversive when their focus is elsewhere. When every discussion points in one direction, it's easy to understand why SSMs feel they are offering something incomplete. We focus on connectedness rather than identity – how far SSMs are 'committed' to the Church, not the totality of their ministry. In summary, SSMs are most affirmed for what they are not and least for what they are.

SSM is sometimes therefore seen as a means to ministry, not an end. Many SSMs disagree – SSM is what they are called to do. It is, based on their gifts and experience, what they are *for*. Given that some people still think SSM is a consolation prize or an unhappy compromise, this needs to be repeated. We should begin by openly questioning unvoiced assumptions, challenging the far from subtle pressures placed on SSMs to disengage from paid work and 'finally' commit to 'full-time' ministry. Congregations certainly need to shake off the idea that SSM is a temporary and unhappy state clergy pass through before they move to stipendiary status.

As this book demonstrates, some clergy work on a self-supporting basis because they are already doing things that matter. That's a thought that needs unpacking. First, although the Church knows that many have a vocation, it's often hard for it to see that a vocation might be centred on another sphere of work – and harder still to understand that ordination might enhance and complement it. For example, many teachers are ordained (and they are not all RE teachers or school chaplains). For some, the vocation to teach is as important as a vocation to minister. Both are 'Christian' vocations. It would not even be true to say that one is ministry and one is a more generalized calling. Many SSMs talk about the fact that every part of their life is ministry – family, community, work and church. In practice some work sectors (teaching and medicine, for example) are seen as more closely aligned to ministry. Selectors sometimes struggle to understand how SSMs might feel called to industry, banking or manufacturing.

We need to remind ourselves that SSM is not shaped by inadequacy. It's not a question of not making the grade or not fully committing. Sometimes what people can offer is limited by necessity, but that does not diminish the offer. After all, ministry is who we are, not the roles we occupy. Being a minister involves a heightened awareness of everything else we do as life partner, family member, householder, parent governor, consumer, student, voter, reader, cinema-goer, jogger, team sports player, trade union member, elected representative or pensioner.

Connecting different worlds

Some SSMs make a positive decision to remain in what the Church describes as 'secular' employment. As Chapter 6 outlines, that adjective 'secular' carries weight. It suggests a distinction between what is inside and what is outside – what is perceived as the heart of ministry and what is seen as peripheral. Those dioceses who offer website information about SSM (many still don't) usually say something relatively affirming about the fact that some ministers have day jobs. An impartial observer might conclude that this work is a recognized aspect of ministry, but that's not how it feels in practice. In choosing to minister (if only some of the time) in the secular world, many SSMs feel they're operating in the space the Church finds least interesting.

Why? It's not because the Church has anything against its clergy having a broader ministry – they are encouraged into all kinds of informal community roles. It is simply a matter of what's on the main agenda. As with other denominations, keeping the show on the road dominates the discussion. As a result, we have lost focus on why SSMs are present, what they do and why they find it important. Even though there are proportionally more SSMs around, it's assumed that what they want to talk about is what the Church needs. SSMs are, quite simply, rarely asked about their ministry outside church. Margaret Whipp describes the SSM as 'an important boundary figure':

> From this perspective, she can discern God's activity in some surprising places. She asks the question, 'what does God look like if you don't start in church?', and finds some very interesting answers. Because she is at home in the secular environment, she can speak with a natural voice, and share the journey of faith with others whose starting point may be far removed from the Church . . . within the trusting relationships that develop among close colleagues, where pastoral care is shared over the coffee machine rather than across the communion rail, the NSM is an accessible focus of God's loving presence.
>
> (Witcombe, 2012, p. 18)

Whipp points to those roles SSMs fulfil, including being 'an interpreter of the church to the world, and of the world to the church' and a conveyer of 'down-to-earth theology and ethics'. This is, of course, by no means exclusive to SSMs, but a key characteristic of their ministry. Here is Gill Mack again: 'As a Minister in Secular Employment I am not in midwifery to convert but to convey Christ' (Francis and Francis, 1998, p. 328).

Where SSMs operate 'at the edge' this is not just a reflection of where they fit into the organization, but a fundamental aspect of being ordained. David Hoyle writes: 'ordained ministry is awkward, controversial, and human . . . We do need clergy who in their glorious, infuriating diversity and peculiarity can help us see past them to a Kingdom that we can share' (Hoyle, 2016, pp. 81–2).

Strengths required by SSMs

More attention could be given to the skills and characteristics required by SSMs. Many of these are required by all clergy, but there are distinctive ingredients.

1 Interpersonal skills

SSMs needs to work within a team, usually led by someone else. Associate ministry requires enormous diplomacy, tact and the ability to convey difficult messages loyally. SSMs need to 'manage upwards' (anticipating a colleague's needs, not displaying the kind of behaviours shown in *Yes, Minister*). The best approach often involves stepping out of the limelight, applying expertise and knowledge sparingly, and giving colleagues space to work in their own style. SSMs also need communication skills to explain what they do (see Chapter 7). As well as the ability to transmit information neutrally and loyally, it helps to know how to be more of a critical friend than a critic, building up rather than tearing down ('appreciative enquiry' provides important tools for this purpose).

2 Managing time

SSMs are often pretty good at time management because of their blended responsibilities. Many understand that multitasking is something of a myth – it usually means you do at least one thing badly. Setting priorities comes first – these may be about work, family life, health and rest, as well as ministry. If your parish time is limited, give it where it's most useful, rather than responding by habit (going to the same routine meetings) or impulse (responding to one emergency after the next). Priority-setting means, sometimes, looking for hard outcomes. If your goal is to begin a new and important project, for example, it's worth regularly asking whether each choice you make moves you closer to a start date.

Managing yourself and your commitments means setting boundaries – and recognizing when you cross them. Watch for early signs of stress and overwork. If you're in paid work as well as ministry you will need to conserve and focus energy. Sometimes you will have to address the overall balance of life to allow space for your calling. Finally, learn how to say 'no' wisely but also diplomatically – you add to urban myths about SSMs if you keep saying, 'Because I'm an SSM I don't . . .'.

3 Taking control of your own ministry development

The case studies in this book reinforce a comment made by many SSMs: where they have found opportunities for personal development, they've often had to identify, negotiate and resource this learning for themselves. Diocesan programmes can be both helpful and relevant, and national and regional events are sometimes on offer. It's still realistic to understand that a fulfilled SSM ministry may require you to take control of your learning agenda. Passively waiting for learning to be offered is unlikely to work. Being a lifelong learner means stretching yourself in different ways. Explore different ways of learning. This might mean shadowing other ministers, working with a mentor and learning new skills. Chapter 10 offers a range of ideas.

4 Resilience

Operating on the edge can sometimes feel like a lonely space. While all clergy risk burnout where they experience relentless pressure, SSMs can sometimes feel a particular kind of disconnected isolation – neither fully inside church not understood outside it. In *Steel Angels* Magdalen Smith writes of the need for clergy to be 'people of resilience, working and living with a backbone of steel', so they remain 'symbols of irrepressible hope for others who have little or none' (Smith, 2014, p. 8). Resilience is, fortunately, not simply hard-wired

into personality. We can acquire it and find strategies that pro
it. For SSMs this is often about finding opportunities for supp
from colleagues in similar roles, and wisdom from a mentor who has
insights into the demands of this form of ministry.

SSM in practice

Hugh Valentine, worker priest

How and why I became an SSM

I had an unexpected and sudden sense that I might be being invited to
serve as a priest. Soon after that I was aware of *not* believing this translated to traditional forms of church-attached, paid, ordained life. It was
the mid-1980s, I was a social worker in London. That, for me, was also
a vocation, and any sense of priestly vocation had arisen, for me, in the
context of that work. Why cleave the two apart? I have always had an
interest in how the gospel relates to lived human experience – the vast
majority of which occurs beyond the church-as-building. And that's
where I wanted to locate myself.

My experience of SSM

I don't like the term SSM and don't use it. For the past 30 years I have
served the Church as a priest, with a primary focus on so-called secular
work.

My experience as a priest in work places beyond the parish

It has sometimes been difficult and lonely. I spent many years in social
services in London – nearly always fiercely secular and anti-Christianity
(but pro other faiths). To deal first with the easy exclusions. Being a
priest while fully immersed in secular work settings has not meant wear-
ing clerical dress at work; it has not meant running lunchtime prayer
meetings. It has meant: taking the office of priest into some of the ordinary working situations of our day, in a way that parish-based clergy and
chaplains to organizations simply cannot; it has been (this may be cited
as a weakness by many) 'invisible', involving the practice of a disguised
dimension of prayer and effort and presence and purpose. I routinely
regarded my desk and working day as an altar. The work which crossed
it in my various roles as social worker, team manager, principal officer,
director, all this I viewed as the very same material handled at the altar –
the stuff of God's promises, of our redemption, of the incarnation of

God into the material facts of our short lives. It has also meant a kind of identification (one could say solidarity), by which I mean something connected with helping the God of the Church-as-institution escape the confines of that institution and be witnessed to in (some of) the myriad circumstances of ordinary lived life. Without doubt, my experience of MSE has been an adventure.

My experience as a priest in the Church

Unpaid clergy don't comfortably fit within the model we have. The Church of England has moved to using greater and greater numbers of unpaid clergy as a response to staffing needs and limited money. This has been divorced from any theological grounds, such as those (still compelling after all these years) that led to the worker priest movement in France. I have been hugely fortunate to be attached to a progressive parish that has supported my interests and has nourished me.

What's the main focus of my ministry?

It is not *my* ministry, but Jesus Christ's, in which I seek to participate. But to answer the question: there are two, equal and complementary areas: the Church-as-institution (in the parishes I have served) and whatever paid work setting I've been in.

Support and training

I have had to arrange my own support and networks. None has been offered by the institution that has been relevant to my work.

Challenges and difficulties

The greatest challenges have arisen within the organizations I have worked for. It soon dawned on me that it is the organizations of our day, more than anything else, which embody the 'powers and principalities' spoken of in the Bible. Practically speaking, the main challenges and difficulties of MSE are balancing demands and coping with tiredness. I have always made it a priority to say 'yes' to as many parish requests as have been made. I have wanted to be a net benefit, not someone who is of little practical value.

Another has been the loneliness of the MSE role. Most SSMs have no interest in being MSEs and, with the wider Church, have little interest in the ordinary working lives of those beyond the institution's borders. I regret that priests with MSE/worker priest focus are poorly equipped by our training and formation and little helped in the task by the Church or its salaried theologians.

The best thing about SSM

The distance it gives in relation to the Church-as-institution. This is not about licence or disobedience but about detachment and independence. The very best thing is knowing that I have been faithful to my vocation, however well or poorly I have discharged it.

I am certain the MSE/worker priest model is a valid strand within the Church's ministerial priesthood. I have no doubt that the worker priests in France in the 1940s and 1950s were correct in their analysis – theological and social – which obliged them to minister not 'to' working people but to take up places alongside them, on the same terms and in the same conditions, the better to carry the good news to them and the better to understand it themselves and for the church.

Looking forward

Now there's a question. I think I'll pass.

6

Some theological resonances

This chapter explores the theology prompted by different understandings of self-supporting ministry.

SSMs and the theology of priesthood

You could fill a modest-sized library with books on the theology of priesthood. Most make the unspoken assumption that their subject is stipendiary and running a parish. Some recent books on Anglican ministry (including works by David Hoyle and Justin Lewis-Anthony) hint at a nostalgia for simpler times before ministries 'offering us more acronyms than we easily remember: SSMs, MSEs and OLMs' (Hoyle, 2016, p. 13).[1]

Church communities sometimes find SSMs theologically challenging. SSMs look like insiders in the sense that they wear special clothing, are called 'Reverend' and are licensed by a bishop. Nevertheless, they are not employed by the Church and give attention to causes outside it. This is even more confusing if they hold down a full-time job that seems to have little connection to church life.

Anyone reflecting on the theology of unpaid clergy encounters opposing realities. First, equality is affirmed with disarming simplicity: a deacon is a deacon; a priest is a priest. At face value, this is encouraging. However, as Chapter 2 outlined, the idea that 'we treat all clergy equally' sometimes means we stop listening to stories and experiences. Often it feels as if difference is tolerated rather than built on. Robin Gill argues that 'non-stipendiary ministry, far from being a theologically indefensible development . . . is actually able to contribute to our theological understanding of ministry as a whole' (Francis and Francis, 1998, p. 267). It would, of course, be foolish to suggest that SSMs are theologically different. As Magdalen Smith writes in *Steel Angels*, 'priesthood does not come wrapped in neat boxes' (Smith, 2014, p. xiv). SSMs are varied in their background, skills and focus of ministry. They are also called to a range of tasks and contexts. This variety is sometimes seen as problematic in terms of deployment, but it is part of the fullness they offer.

Pointing beyond

We probably need more theology around ministries focused on life outside the parish. Michael Bourke writes: 'All the classic definitions of priesthood are in terms of the leadership of the Christian community.' He sees the worker priest as being on a 'voyage of discovery', facing key questions: 'In what way will ordination help him minister more effectively in an environment which is by definition "non-church"? . . . How does he relate to the worshipping community and its central eucharistic act?' Bourke concludes:

> we have to admit that we do not possess a ready-made theology of the church into which we can fit an equally prefabricated doctrine of priesthood. The church cannot be simply identified with the parish family at the Lord's Table on the Lord's Day . . . There is a theological need for exploration, for pluralism of approach. The task of the worker-priest is to live at this frontier, to discover what faith is and what it means to be a disciple in the secular world and to seek out the church there, without denying the church back home.
>
> (Francis and Francis, 1998, pp. 270–6)

Bourke's reflection sees a balance – 'finding church' elsewhere, 'without denying the church back home'. This balancing act accurately describes what many SSMs experience, feeling that they operate in a 'twilight zone' between being priests at work and 'helping out in the parish'. When little institutional attention is given to one area of ministry, feelings of disconnection increase. There is much to unpack here and it probably needs a refreshed theological perspective. SSMs need, repeatedly, to justify what they do outside church – to explain how what they do is relevant, useful and priestly. The challenges they hear are daunting. Not just, 'What are you doing to grow the congregation?' but 'Why do you need to be ordained for your ministry at work?' We appear to have lost a great deal of Bourke's sense of 'finding church' in our efforts to keep church going.

Even so, calling in, bringing people to faith, encouraging regular church attendance – these are important benchmarks. Affirming community is part of the ordained minister's call, not just to fill pews but because believing and belonging (to take the modern sociological terms) are intertwined. David Hoyle writes: 'Christ summons us into the Kingdom, and a kingdom is a place where people live together. Our unity matters.' He adds: 'At the heart of Christian vocation is an absolute determination to point away from ourselves' (Hoyle, 2016, pp. 54 and 57).

Rowan Williams delivered a lecture at Cuddesdon in May 2004 in celebration of Michael Ramsey's *The Christian Priest Today*.[2] Williams suggests that one of the responsibilities of the priest is to be a 'lookout, telling unwelcome truths', and also to be an 'interpreter' – 'by which I mean not primarily someone who interprets culture to and for the Church or interprets the Church's teaching to the world outside, but someone who has the gift of helping people make sense to and of each other'. Drawing people into community, and celebrating where community already exists, is for a larger reason – hope. This, too, is where clergy point, often in contexts where hope is most needed.

Such metaphors – pointing, being a signpost and interpreter – are where a theology of SSM might take us. A clear function of priesthood is to be sign and signal, pointing to something beyond ourselves. Is this role different for SSMs? How is it exercised where God-language is off the agenda? These are big questions, explored in some of the case studies in this book. For many SSMs, being a signpost feels like a very different role. For example, talking about the kingdom to those who don't 'speak church' requires a different language. One of the distinctive things about MSEs and SSMs is that they are less likely to use the insider code of religious language when preaching. This is not about being fashionably contemporary, but fulfilling the Book of Common Prayer requirement to 'set forth thy true and lively Word' – bringing text to life.

Liminal ministry

Chapter 5 explored ministry at the margins; this isn't a new idea, but it's central. Being salt, light or yeast is about being part of society but also acting separately on it – being an observer, an agent of change, as well as a participant. The edge has always been an important place to be for those who speak truth to power, those who need to shake things up. Working on the margins is not only vital; for many SSMs it's the right place to be. Knowing this doesn't make it any more comfortable. This discomfort, if you like, is a cost of ministry not often explored, but it *is* a cost. Many SSMs feel on the back foot a great deal of the time, needing to justify, explain, sometimes to apologize. This may well be the primary cost that SSMs accept as part of their calling – to be undefined, vulnerable to challenge. However, even a blinkered comment opens a potentially rich conversation. Redefining ministry is one way we rethink church.

Preaching on the fiftieth anniversary of the first ordinations from the Southwark Ordination Course, Steven Croft celebrated three important qualities in SSMs: generosity, humility and liminality. Croft argues that SSMs offer a 'gift of time' in terms of vocational preparation, training and, of course, ministry. For Croft this is shaped by humility: 'Those who serve in this way have to offer what they can, constrained by time and circumstances, and offer what is needed. They are not caught up in temptations to ambition or influence.' Croft outlines the third quality, liminality, as follows:

> this new form of priesthood is shaped by liminality: by living permanently on the edge and between two or more worlds. This can be a blessing. It can also be complex and demanding as many here will know. But it is a precious gift to the wider church and has many lessons for a church in mission . . . the liminality at the heart of self-supporting ministry calls for anchoring and security on the part of the wider church. It is always difficult to live between two worlds. One of the things you need are secure lines of connexion and accountability which are both personal and institutional. As all the research indicates, self-supporting ministers are not self-supporting in this sense: they need support from their bishops and dioceses in order to sustain this edgy and liminal pattern of priesthood which is so vital for God's mission.[3]

Liminal ministry is not confined to SSMs. Other clergy, especially chaplains, find themselves in similar places. Martyn Percy explores priesthood in these terms:

> Clergy, to function as effective ministers, often discover their role and tasks to be about becoming central in the more marginal and ambiguous moments of life. Clergy occupy that

strange hinterland between the secular and the sacred, the temporal and eternal, acting as interpreters and mediators, embodying and signifying faith, hope and love. They are both distant and immediate, remote yet intimate. And in occupying this most marginal and transitory ground, sometimes helping to close the gaps between these worlds, they become humanly and spiritually necessary even as they live out their (partly willed, partly imposed) social marginality. It is a unique yet evolving paradigm . . . To be of the people; but also for their sake, to be wholly other.

(Percy, 2006, pp. 73–4)

Percy's description of 'marginal and transitory ground' speaks powerfully to SSMs.

Operating in unholy territory

Let's revisit the word 'secular'. It's a key word for MSEs, obviously, but matters to SSMs with a ministry outside church. Often we use the word 'secular' to indicate hostility to religion. The National Secular Society defines secularism as the 'strict separation of the state from religious institutions', ensuring that 'people of different religions and beliefs are equal before the law'. Christian communities use the word in other ways. Sometimes it neutrally describes the broader world of commerce, industry, economics and politics where the Church is sometimes heard or present – parts of human experience with the potential to be redeemed. Sometimes it refers to people who are currently 'unchurched' (an extraordinarily territorial term). Often 'secular' is used as a synonym for 'godless'. The phrase 'secular values' is rarely used positively in church. It's easy to believe that much in our culture is either irrelevant to God or actively gets in the way of his purposes. 'Secular' has become the opposite of 'sacred'.

All this is theologically and historically illiterate. 'Secular' has its roots in the Latin for 'generation' or 'age', therefore relating to things that are worldly and temporal. The term was used to describe clergy based in a parish rather than those living in monasteries. We might perhaps listen more carefully to those who write about the 'myth of secularisation'.[4] Alternatively we could reflect on the Collect for the Sixth Sunday after Trinity: 'Pour into our hearts such love toward you, that we, loving you in all things and above all things, may obtain your promises.'[5] Remembering this says 'in' as well as 'above' is the first step towards finding God where he is working, rather than where we have confined him.

It's narrow, to say nothing of sloppy, theological thinking to think of the secular world as godless. We seem to have lost some of the eagerness of past generations to find God in contemporary life, and we may also have lost sight of the way Church and society learn from each other. After all, it does sometimes feel (heresy of heresies) that in some areas 'Church' learns from 'world' – most recently, some would argue, in relation to human equality and diversity.

Human beings are good at binary thinking – deciding what is clean or unclean, sacred or profane. In the UK, vicious 'trolling' on social media, and even death threats, have become frighteningly common. Polarized views abound when people feel frightened – as headline readers in our 'post-truth' world recognize. Where erecting walls feels more important than providing a welcome, we drift into a tired 'us and them' theology. Then a community moves from feeling it is right to losing the capacity to believe it can ever be wrong. Talking about 'inside' and 'outside' endorses tribalism. Anthony Stevens argues that war and conflict often arise from our capacity for 'pseudo-speciation' – an ability to treat other races, nations or communities as non-human: 'We possess an inherent propensity to regard ourselves as superior and to treat the members of communities other than our own as if they belonged to inferior species' (Stevens, 2004, p. 43). Christian communities should always find binary thinking not just uncomfortable but alien. Jesus disrupted unimaginative conformity and challenged closed systems of thinking. He infuriated hardliners by telling parables – fluid, open-ended stories requiring us to participate rather than just listen. More than ever, the role of churches is to model reflection and a calm inclusiveness.

Suspicion of the secular can make us question the value of what SSMs do outside the parish. This relates closely to what those 'in here' think and feel about what's 'out there'. Institutions under stress respond like human beings, becoming more self-protecting; a frightened Church is easily persuaded that God is exclusive. We pray for 'the Church and the world', not thinking much about the overlap. Congregations hope new people will come to church, but show little interest in how God is already working in those people's lives. Are we sent out at the end of the Eucharist to draw others in or to meet Christ in them where they are? If the latter, could we do more, theologically and practically, for outward-facing clergy?

The most basic theology primer explains that creation is a gift: God made the world, liked what he had made and shared it with us to care for and enjoy. That simple narrative is, of course, disrupted, but creation is still a sign of God's blessing. We prepare the table in *Common Worship* saying, 'everything in heaven and on earth is yours. All things come from you, and of your own do we give you.'[6] Everything. All things. And yet many Christians seem not to believe these words. We use Scripture to adopt a position – being *in* the world but not *of* the world. This absolutism seems to make perfect sense when you're dealing with society from a distance, but makes no sense at all to congregation members trying to be faithful Christians in messy, complicated lives. Finding God in all things challenges orthodoxy, but affirms, in Marcus Borg's words, that, 'The ineffable, the sacred, is real and present' (Borg, 1997, p. 49); or as Jürgen Moltmann argues, 'To experience God in all things presupposes that there is a transcendence which is immanent in things . . . It is the infinite in the finite, the eternal in the temporal, and the enduring in the transitory' (Moltmann, 1992, p. 35).

As a curate I was much inspired by the 'After Sunday' movement[7] championed by Peter Sinclair. In the vestry I pinned up an image taken from one of Peter's workshops – a Teesside chemical plant with venting towers dominating the skyline. Underneath, a printed question: 'Where do you see God in this picture?' (not 'Do you?' but 'Where do you?'). This picture challenges our assumption that God is present only in certain places. We're immediately happy to think of God's presence in a beautiful landscape, a sunset, running water or in a quiet space. We are conditioned not to look for God where life is busy, noisy, industrial or chaotic. Believing that God is only in church, whether you mean the building or the institution, is a way of deciding where God is absent. How do we have any right to decide where God is *not*?

Scripture tells us that God takes the most unpromising people and situations and makes them shine. Some have found God to be most present at times of utmost discomfort, in hardship or where humanity is seen at its ugliest. If this is a God in whom we live and breathe and have our being, why on earth would we try to persuade ourselves that God is absent from selected areas of experience? Just as we constantly limit God by recreating him in our own image, we incessantly tell him where he is not supposed to be. A deeper tradition argues that God *is*, full stop. Our job is to seek and to recognize.

Finding 'heaven in ordinary' is central to many SSMs who point to God's presence in the ordinary stuff of life. This is why metaphors of liminality abound. SSMs help to redefine ministry because they have important opportunities to rediscover what God is doing, encouraging dialogue between the familiar and the unknown. SSMs, among others, redefine what we mean by 'secular', interpret it and sometimes bless it. This is perhaps what Gill Mack means when she suggests 'a minister in secular employment must learn to be part of the church in its invisible form' (Francis and Francis, 1998, p. 325). That invisible form is potentially more useful than we remember. Making connections reveals new angles, new truths.

Celebrating God's universal presence means giving people new reasons to follow and belong. It's not a gimmick, but attention to the raw intensity of our gospel. Properly connecting with the world we pray for provokes fresh language and thinking. If society has lost interest in what we loosely term 'organized religion', we should take note of an idea expressed recently by Bishop Robert Atwell – newcomers to church are looking for 'organized informality' but what we usually give them is 'disorganized formality' (Atwell, 2013, p. 5).

SSM in practice

Gillian White, SSM pioneer, Derby Diocese

How and why I became an SSM

I have been in SSM for ten years. I always felt called to serve in *both* church and work. However, I was ordained into a church context where there were no full-time clergy and plenty of ministerial demands, so I have always focused on church as well as work. I've had two different kinds of vocation in two separate but interconnected areas of life and that has blurred the edges of my vocation and made it richer. It's grown and changed over time as well, and continues to do so.

My experience of SSM

When I was ordained I was a clinical dietitian working as a therapy services manager within the NHS, and I continued in that role through my curacy and for about three years afterwards. There were crossover opportunities, but I was always clear that I was in a clinical role and not working as a chaplain. There are quite a few ordained ministers working in the NHS outside chaplaincy. One of the interesting roles I had was to be on the Ethics Committee for the hospital. There were no tensions but a lot of 'working things out'. Work gave me experience of things like working with others and coping with change which were helpful in church too. Church kept me in touch with people on the ground and how God values them. In my diocese I have undertaken a dozen face-to-face interviews with SSMs, which has made me deeply aware of the variety of experiences within the SSM community. Some are very church-based, others have a clear workplace focus, some are mixed as I was.

What's the main focus of my ministry?

I am now mostly retired from my NHS role and the focus of my ministry today is very much in church. My role is engaging with the wider community in order to help the church reimagine itself. I'm currently an associate minister licensed as SSM pioneer in Tideswell, in Derby Diocese. A great deal of what I can put into this role arises from my experience of workplace ministry, and specifically from experiences that I would not have gained if I'd been an incumbent.

Support and training

When I was in training there was still a strong sense of what it meant to have a 'proper' clergy role. There was a spread of helpfulness towards SSMs, but an underlying sense that stipendiary ministry was the proper way. I'd also have to say that there was not a lot of understanding presented about self-supporting ministry or how we could prepare for it in practical terms. Even so, my training experience was very good. I enjoyed discussion groups where the SSM voice could be heard and opportunities to look at the realities of SSM (for example, when you might wear a dog collar at work and how you might deal with the funeral of a colleague). I valued the chance to offer a theological reflection based on my professional role in the workplace.

My curacy was a very good experience. It took a little while to find the right place to serve but I was helped by my bishop to find an appropriate church where SSMs were already in place. That made a big difference; I felt valued for who I was and what I could offer, not just as a part-time extra.

Continuing ministerial education has been flexible and helpful, but it's very church focused and there are few opportunities to reflect on workplace ministry. There was nothing about being an SSM curate and how you grow into associate ministry, which is important for all clergy to think about.

Challenges and difficulties

One positive challenge for SSMs is that you often have to make your own connections and to negotiate your own learning pathways. For too long the Church has had a 'one-size-fits-all' mindset as far as training and development are concerned. I'm sure this will change as we see a greater variety of ministry and more reliance on SSMs.

A more difficult challenge is the way that people simply don't 'get' workplace ministry – including some other SSMs! Some people in the Church continue to see stipendiary ministry as 'better' rather than 'different'. We therefore continue to find incumbents who don't understand what their SSM colleagues have to offer and feel threatened by them. I find it grates that at times we waste potential and demoralize talented ministers as a result.

The best thing about SSM

What I enjoy most is making connections between work and church, as well as building links. Working at the coalface means that you are where people outside church spend most of their time. You can also make stronger connections with working people in your church communities as you share similar experiences. I try to recognize this when I'm leading worship and in preaching. I love the variety of ways that we can serve as priests and, as an SSM, I have an important freedom to do different things and to experiment.

Looking forward

For me, the important thing about growing as an SSM is finding an integrated way of being a priest – *all* of who I am. One SSM colleague talked about the gift that SSMs offer of being 'bilingual'. We can translate. The language of the world is spoken here as well as the language of church.

7

SSM conversations

Communication – the essentials

Communication is at the heart of ministry. We are given a message of hope and that message has to get through. Unsurprisingly, therefore, preaching and teaching are high on the agenda for ministers. Which is not to say that clergy are universally good public speakers or adult educators, but compared to many other professions most take active steps to maintain and improve skills in this area.

Communication also matters as a means of building relationships with congregations and teams. What most job descriptions for parish positions require is the ability to communicate a 'vision'. Like many things in church, this is more talked about than implemented. Visionary leadership is evident, but hard to maintain. Often the bar is set unrealistically high; clergy feel under pressure to shape and direct the communities they serve and are often told to be 'more visionary'. In practice, of course, persuading any group of volunteers to change their worldview or behaviours radically is a hurdle where many stumble.

The Church can learn from the anxieties of the business world as well as from its best practice. In business, too, visionary language is overused and often emptied of meaning. Business leaders experience guilt that they have not managed to fully articulate a vision, craft the right kind of vision statement or motivate team members towards shared goals. In business and in church there are small victories, sustained periods of growth and times that might feel like stagnation but may simply be quieter times when things settle in.

Nevertheless, shaping some kind of vision matters. Creating and holding on to a big idea makes a group feel purposeful and optimistic. SSMs have a role to play in idea-building, contributing ideas and encouragement, being positive team members and, most of all, not getting in the way of progress (see further discussion of associate leadership in Chapter 10).

Communication within teams

Clergy are often judged by their ability to communicate warmth, empathy, good teaching and big ideas. However, on the ground what matters is *information*. Keeping people up to date, informed, making them feel appreciated and part of the picture – achieving this is the everyday adhesive that binds working communities. It's the most mundane kind of communication and therefore sometimes neglected. Good practice points to successful contexts where communication works in three ways. So among ministry team members, communication needs to be:

1 **regular** even if it seems repetitive, information has to flow in a predictable cycle;
2 **consistent** it disturbs colleagues if you share minute details about some projects and others happen unannounced;
3 **encouraging** don't just describe activities, talk about the good work that has gone into them, give positive responses and praise early results.

The parish priests I work with often put a huge amount of effort into what feels like a constant process – ensuring colleagues are in the loop. Keeping people up to speed makes them feel that their viewpoint matters. Where this is done well, normally you find a leader who instinctively knows the value of regular, clear communication. There are important outcomes – doing your best to ensure no one feels excluded or surprised by developments and as few toes are trodden on as possible. Good communication requires a constant awareness of the inherent propensity within any religious community for misunderstanding and conflict. Where relationships break down the first diagnosis offered is usually 'the vicar doesn't communicate' or 'things aren't delegated' (one of the costs of parish leadership is that any communication problem is the incumbent's fault, but when things run smoothly few people notice). However, it should never just be the nominated leader who manages this process and maintains tone.

Losing the motivation to keep communicating is a problem. People working under pressure tend to withdraw into themselves, are more likely to act without consulting and start to believe it's easier to get on and do the job than explain it to someone else. A huge amount has been written about delegation in churches, but the advice offered rarely reflects the actual pressures experienced by clergy. Delegating isn't just about communicating, it's about supporting and nurturing, which take large amounts of time. That's why encouragement matters so much. The most effective forms of communication consider the emotional life of the listener as well as the information contained in the message. So, for example, if you are consulting the congregation about significant change it's vital to understand that ideas are rarely seen objectively. Also, if the idea isn't yours, it can be very tempting to subtly undermine change.

All ministers in a team have a responsibility to emphasize the positive. That doesn't mean glossing over failure or disappointment or walking round with an unconvincing fixed smile, but it's important to be a messenger of hope. This means building a culture where every team member vocalizes energy and warmth. Accentuating the positive (or at least looking for it) sounds hackneyed, but it's all too often absent in church teams. Where praise and encouragement are threaded into the daily round of announcements this has a measurable effect. Effectively, you are coaching communities – to spot things worth affirming and to know how to do so. Hearing praise, as long as it sounds genuine, models something important. It says that the purpose of communication is to build up rather than tear down, to celebrate the bigger picture rather than always getting caught up in the details of implementation.

Communicating as SSMs

Working as an associate minister presents difficulties and opportunities in terms of communication. It's possible to encourage good practice and to be part of it. At times you will see missed opportunities and things that have been communicated badly or late. Occasionally you will get in the way of good communication by sitting on vital information or sharing it selectively. Associate ministers may not entirely set the tone of the parish or congregation, but they help shape it.

As Chapter 9 outlines, loyalty needs to be shown as well as felt. Associate clergy need to self-monitor carefully. If you are generating new ideas, it is vital to understand how these play alongside pre-existing initiatives. It's a subtle balance between respecting your own agenda and being in tune with the rest of the team. At times you will lead from the front and initiate change, but this needs to be done with huge sensitivity. People-watchers have a well-tuned ear for anything that sounds like dissent, so it's vital not just to support colleagues but to show that you do – with visible good grace. Rather than playing devil's advocate, be a critical friend, building on what's going well.

Listen to the way different agendas are expressed in the average church service. One person reads the notices, then someone else might introduce the service. A minister might preach and another voice might preside at the altar. Often a different person leads the intercessions. These voices can offer a harmonized picture of the church and its purpose or can present views in conflict. How many times have you heard church notices or intercessions that are a thinly veiled criticism of the incumbent's latest strategy?

Associate clergy sit close to the leader's table, if not at it. Therefore the communication styles they adopt matter. Associate ministry is a privileged position with influence, which means possessing the power to support or undermine. SSMs (and retired clergy) who have served in a community for many years sometimes adopt unhelpful positions when new incumbents arrive. What seems at first to be respectful cooperation can turn into passive-aggressive opposition. The associate minister only has to hint that things aren't what they used to be and the new incumbent's plans are seriously dented. Opposition can be justified in all kinds of ways – you're maintaining tradition, saddened by incompetence or claiming that someone needs to speak for the parish. In reality, someone whose duty is to pass messages on without prejudice adds unhelpful 'spin'.

Within the world of coaching, a term is used to describe the risk of reshaping information when we pass it on. Coaching aims for 'clean language', where there is no agenda, no emotional nuance. Perfection here is impossible, but it's possible to set the bar high. When summarizing what a client says, a coach uses language that is as 'clean' as possible – for example, 'What I'm hearing sounds like anger', rather than, 'Why are you so angry?' When passing on opinions, it requires enormous care to present them objectively, choosing language that gives no hint of your own feelings. That doesn't mean that all information should be presented neutrally – if you're passing on a good idea backed by a number of people, simple loyalty requires you to convey enthusiasm. If you are passing on a complaint, however, it will be necessary to work at communicating 'clean' informational content, without emotional colouring (or your personal 'concerns', which might throw petrol on the fire).

Clean language is vital in associate ministry. It means thinking carefully about the emotional impact of what you say. It means planning sensitively how and when something is communicated. If in doubt, one to one is always the preferred option for difficult news and often the best means of taking soundings. People value some private space in which to react to something difficult or to respond to the affirmation that comes from being sought out for their expertise.

Difficult conversations

It's worth thinking about how to say difficult things, particularly to colleagues. 'Difficult' covers many situations, but one key aspect is the emotional outcome. It pays to be realistic about the change of mood you are likely to create, even in an audience of one. Thirty years ago I worked alongside a highly effective middle school head teacher in Surrey who was a skilled people manager. I asked him how he worked and he told me about his mental preparation. He would carefully prepare not just what he was going to say, but how it would be heard. He imagined the recipient's actual reply. Too many leaders state that they are not responsible for the way their messages are received. The opposite is true: each of us is entirely responsible for the outcomes we create. This doesn't mean that we have total control over the way other people respond, but it does mean that any communication begins with the listener's perspective in mind.

When it comes to teams, committees and working groups, tone matters as much as outcomes. Often, for example, the way a PCC operates is more important than the things it decides on. Tone affects the way people hear things in a group, when we're highly attuned to the reactions of others. Some want their feelings to be heard, so dominate the discussion; others work hard to ensure they give nothing away (this is often the person who sends you difficult emails at midnight, three hours after a meeting has apparently ended in consensus). With all meetings it's important to be clear from the outset what ground rules are in play.

Whoever leads or facilitates discussions – and SSMs should be deeply involved in both processes – it's helpful to say what kind of thinking is required. If you're helping a colleague manage a difficult meeting, try to clarify what process is involved. Is the group's function to brainstorm, to listen or to act? If the matter is urgent then pragmatic decisions are required. If you're discussing long-term change (particularly changes to hearts and minds), jumping quickly into decision-making mode encourages fixed positions. Is the main purpose of the meeting to reflect or to plan? Is the process about idea-building, problem-solving or build-ing support for something already decided? Is a meeting required at all – would one-to-one conversations work better? Transparency about process is vital, but this is often missing from PCC meetings, where the most difficult issues are often parked towards the time of the evening when impatience will be highest and minds most closed.

Consultation is in vogue, but largely misunderstood. Church teams constantly speculate about what 'people out there' are thinking, but it's relatively easy to find out. Questionnaires and surveys are no better than the weakest question posed and always represent an agenda. Try a focus group. This is a gathering of individuals from your commu-nity (think consumers rather than committee members – talk to the kind of individuals you hope to engage, including fringe members, rather than people whose views are well known). Explain that the meeting is to gather thoughts rather than make decisions – there are no wrong answers and anything can be said. Find a neutral facilitator who does not represent an identifiable interest group. Ask open ques-tions: 'What have you seen?' 'How did it feel?' Ask what people would like to see in the future and what that would look and feel like. In one focus group I listened to, fringe members talked movingly about how daunting it can feel to open the heavy wooden church door without knowing what's on the other side, suggesting that glass doors are more inviting. Rather than driving your own agenda with questions like, 'Would you welcome a service for young families?', ask how people currently experience what you offer, if something would work better and what shape that might take.

Explaining SSM

There is one other context where communication matters to SSMs – wherever you're given the opportunity to explain your role. Chapter 1 outlined the way SSMs face questions such as 'You're not a proper vicar, then?' There are two perspectives on this – frustration and opportunity.

Frustration first. SSM can lead to feeling like a fringe member of the clergy tribe. Operating in more than one world can mean that you never feel fully attached or accepted in either. You might, for example, serve as a priest in a local parish, but also work full time in a context that is different, geographically and in other ways. Clergy in this situation talk about opportunities, too – the rewards and difficulties of bridge ministry (see Chapter 7). Clearly, SSMs can bring something distinctive, if not unique, to both contexts. The SSM who is grounded in the world of work is often well equipped to bring the concerns of the wider world into worship and preaching, and will have opportunities to discuss faith issues outside the boundaries of the parish. A spiritual director once said to me that the Church has a great need for those who hang on to ministry 'by the edge of their fingertips'. The downside of this bridge ministry is that sometimes SSMs feel they no longer fit comfortably into the workplace and, at the same time, their identity within the Church is fragile.

Explaining MSE

MSEs, too, have challenges and opportunities. Even though we have had MSEs for over half a century, they still puzzle congregations (and more than occasionally some senior clergy). If the work you do outside church can be labelled chaplaincy, that makes immediate sense; in a way, you're a minister on loan – 'doing church' but on someone else's premises. If you're embedded in work, an ordained workplace minister doing the same work as your colleagues, you'll regularly face the question, 'Why couldn't you do this as a lay Christian?' Beyond the obvious potential for irritation, the question is, of course, a gift in disguise. It opens doors to people understanding the changing shape of ministry. Even more important, it requires some gentle theological reflection approaching the idea that God might be present in more areas of life than we care to admit.

Hearing and answering this question is part of the sacrificial burden of many SSMs. It's a question that is never put to stipendiary clergy, even if they are doing something entirely un-churchy like chatting in the pub or taking part in a round of bingo. To my knowledge, no one ever knocks on a vicarage door to ask, 'Why did you need to get ordained to do this?' One of the more useful answers to this question comes from John Mantle in his book on the worker priest movement:

A favourite criticism – still heard – and usually couched as a question was: 'what did a worker-priest have to offer in the workplace that layman did not?' The simple answer might be an understanding of human and pastoral problems, substantial theological comprehension and a human face for a distant institution whose clergy he represented. But the question can be put the other way: 'what did an ordained priest have to offer the parish?' If the answer was obviously some kind of 'leadership', a focus of the community's understanding and celebration, why should he not provide the same for those who might one day ask for it somewhere else? To suggest that the working world was the right place for laymen or -women only, and the parish for the parson, was to suggest divided worlds with the parish existing in some other exclusive dimension 'not of this world'.

(Mantle, 2000, pp. 269–70)

MSE in practice

Margaret Trivasse, MSE, Manchester Diocese, NHS counsellor

How and why I became an MSE

I trained on the Northern Ordination Course and was ordained deacon in 2004, serving in Manchester Diocese. I always knew that my primary vocation was to be an ordained person in the workplace.

My experience of MSE

My role is not formally recognized – it can't be, in the NHS. Managers and colleagues know but as far as clients are concerned I can't normally even share the fact that I am a Christian. However, that doesn't mean that my ministry doesn't exist – quite the opposite. It's about being rather than doing, and being is about presence – the love of God flow-ing through me. There are huge parallels between priestly ministry and person-centred counselling with its principles of unconditional positive regard and empathy.

What's the main focus of my ministry?

Working full time in a demanding role means I need to be really clear about my focus of ministry being in work. In a way, I have a vocation within a vocation, because the most important part of my work is working with asylum seekers and refugees. I am licensed to St Gabriel's in Prestwich and preside or preach most Sundays. I'm fortunate to have a congregation who are interested in the work I do and an understanding colleague who recognizes that I have to maintain emotional strength for both roles. I'm pleased to be attached to the C of E but don't have any particular interest in propping it up as an institution. To me the Church seems too interested in itself at the moment, inward-looking rather than engaging with a bigger picture.

Support and training

Virtually all the training or support I've received I've organized for myself, in terms of finding people and organizations. That skill of self-reliance is vital to MSEs. CHRISM's reflective weekends have fed me for many years.

Challenges and difficulties

I'm content to be working on the edge. I have no gripes about not being involved in chapter meetings and so on. I understand that the Church can't always meet the needs of MSEs. My biggest challenge reminds me that MSEs often have prophetic roles – I have to push back on the way the NHS is leaning towards cheaper, more process-driven methods of supporting clients. Cognitive behavioural therapy requires literacy and a certain degree of stability, while other kinds of counselling are being squeezed out by budgets.

The best thing about MSE

I'm supported by congregation members who see me as down to earth and connected with what's happening in society. Having a day job makes people see you differently and encourages them to think about why you're not entirely focused on church. I also recognize that what happens at the altar gives me the strength to do my day job.

Looking forward

MSE works for me because it allows the flexibility for me to focus on the things I feel called to do. My next big question is what happens to MSEs when they retire? I don't want any free time that is created to be swallowed up by a parish, so I may think about retraining and doing something else outside the Church – I don't want to lose the edge I have from being out in the world.

8

Ministers in secular employment

As Chapter 2 outlined, SSM comes in many flavours. Some are MSEs – clergy whose main focus of ministry is their paid work outside the Church of England. This chapter explores their work.

What is an MSE?

'Minister in secular employment' is arguably clearer than some ecclesiastical job titles. Two words out of the three are clear to those who don't 'speak church': 'minister' and 'employment'. Here's a breakdown of how the role relates to other, similar labels.

- **SSMs** often continue in paid work outside the Church after ordination. They may not be known as MSEs. The balance between paid work and church work varies considerably. Some SSMs feel the purpose of paid work is to fund their church ministry. Others feel their ministry outside church is integral to SSM.
- **MSEs** also remain in paid work after ordination, but, whether or not officially licensed as MSEs, their 'main focus of ministry' is the workplace. Nevertheless, nearly all MSEs are also licensed to a parish context. The work they do is an important expression of their calling (where this is the case, some MSEs describe themselves as worker priests).
- **Worker priests** are generally seen to be exclusively focused on the working world, revisiting the European worker priest movement. Worker priests acknowledge important pastoral encounters, but feel their work is their calling rather than the opportunities it provides for workplace ministry. Some are concerned that the title 'worker priest' excludes other denominations and ministries.
- **Workplace chaplains** (or 'industrial' chaplains), some of whom are ordained, can be found in a number of organizations. These chaplains are generally not employed by the organizations they serve. Their role is pastoral engagement rather than doing the same work as other employees.

Workplace chaplain or MSE?

Chaplains in factories, offices, warehouses and shopping centres are not employees of the organizations they serve and their primary role is to be available for pastoral contact. Some are paid by churches, some minister elsewhere, some are volunteers. They usually work out of a chaplaincy office, visiting different parts of the workplace, sometimes leading prayer and discussion groups.

Sometimes MSEs work in the same environment as chaplains. For example, chaplains are present in universities, where there are also ordained university staff in a range of roles. The NHS has paid and unpaid chaplains, whose role is to minister to patients and staff, but it also employs other staff who happen to be ordained. Their job is to minister by *being* medical staff.

Called to work

MSEs are a group within the SSM community. Most work full time, some are self-employed, often in the same work they were doing before they were ordained. MSEs are different from chaplains in terms of role, purpose and visibility. MSEs are not 'parachuted in', as one practitioner described it. They are not chaplains, but the workplace provides extensive opportunities for different forms of ministry. Their role is 'being church' in a different context, facilitating faith conversations that might not otherwise happen. Some MSEs see the main purpose of this as pastoral workplace ministry, but others state categorically that the work they do is their calling. In practice, the two overlap.

Reference to the traditional four-fold picture of ministry might offer insights into the work of MSEs.

1 Their work usually has a **pastoral** element, but one that is defined by 'working alongside' rather than chaplaincy. The MSE's familiarity with the pressures and joys of work provides an important perspective.
2 Their work has a **prophetic** or 'wisdom' dimension to it – supporting, questioning and challenging the values of individuals and organizations, and the decisions they make.
3 They are often **evangelists** in the sense that everyday work contexts naturally provide opportunities to reflect on the gospel. Some

would argue that their presence is a way of *being* gospel. MSEs are often gifted at bringing the language of faith into the workplace and the language of work into worship.

4 They frequently find themselves **teachers** or at least translators, unpacking church thinking, doctrine and the Bible in everyday conversation.

The organization Christians in Secular Ministry (CHRISM, <www.chrism.org.uk>) welcomes members who 'view their paid work in the so-called secular world as the ministry to which they are principally called'. MSEs provide one of the strongest links between church and the world of work, affirming that work itself can be a form of discipleship. In their work they choose to live out the gospel among those who often appear to seek it the least, and to stand up for principles in contexts not normally engaged in conversation with the life of faith. MSEs speak of workplace encounters that celebrate Christ's presence as effectively as any other form of outreach. They do not have special status or duties, but perform the same tasks as others working in the same role. They work to serve an organization and its needs, experiencing the same pressures, frustrations and rewards as their co-workers: 'It will be a ministry partly to the private concerns, the souls, of the people among whom we work but it will also be a ministry in and to the structures of the work, to its processes and to the work itself' (Michael Ranken, in Francis and Francis, 1998, p. 281).

MSEs are found in the full range of work sectors and occupations – in the private, public and third sectors, and in large and small organizations. Some have a ministry focused on supporting colleagues, others talk of a wider ministry to customers or clients. Some work out their calling in relatively isolated work, for example in research; others interact with other people.

Gift and presence

MSEs have concerns about their visibility to the Church. Even so, many acknowledge that their authorized presence is the Church's gift to society. Working alongside means long-term relationships. Since few wear a clerical collar at work, colleagues often discover gradually, sometimes only after deep conversation, that the person they work with is ordained. Being ordained at work may be half-invisible, but it is not a secret ministry – colleagues' curiosity about what MSEs do often sparks interesting exchanges. MSEs' faith is often more evident from who they are than what they say about their beliefs.

Many MSEs speak of a subtle, quiet, but nevertheless valued presence – appreciated by colleagues and by the organization as a whole. MSEs fulfil a representative role by representing church, usually in the most un-churchy way possible. Their roles are also symbolic, pointing to the universal ministry of the baptized, reminding colleagues that 'ministry' doesn't always come with a clerical collar or a church building and being ordained doesn't cut anyone off from ordinary life.

MSEs describe powerful connections between work, prayer and sacrament. They talk about the way work contexts lead naturally to moments of confession, absolution, healing and blessing – even though such religious language may never be used. They speak about how their celebration of the Eucharist reaches out to, informs and incorporates the world of work. Even so, MSEs are acutely aware of the dangers of 'churchifying' the workplace, no longer being seen as a colleague but as a chaplain or visiting vicar. MSEs are called to do their job, the best way they can, alongside others. MSEs do not simply respond to the workplace context; they are embedded in it.

A forgotten motive

By 2000, the year his definitive work was published, John Mantle acknowledged that the British worker priest movement had largely expired, but referred to those who 'continue to strive for a ministry at work ... it is vital to acknowledge the life, work and theology of ministers in secular employment, one group at least who have tried to keep this ministry alive' (Mantle, 2000, p. 274). Mantle saw worker priests and MSEs as rather different species. On one hand, the worker priest movement was focused on ordinary working lives – priests took on manual jobs in industry. MSEs, on the other hand, mainly come from the same middle/professional class as stipendiary clergy; with important exceptions, most work in white-collar jobs, some relatively senior.

When the Church first ordained unpaid clergy in 1963 it was holding two slightly contradictory ideas in tension. The first was to ordain ministers who were firmly embedded in other walks of life. The second was that they would be committed to work *and* church.

These were called 'auxiliary ministers' (the term, interestingly, signalling their main role as supporting parochial clergy). Clergy shortages were not the main driver, but there was a strong interest in ordaining individuals already holding down worthwhile and fulfilling occupations. Half a century on, the balance has tipped towards parish support and for various reasons MSE is not close to the main agenda.

Calling, selection and training

MSEs often find it harder than other ministers to outline their calling. MSEs are perhaps asked why they need to be ordained more than any other clergy. One perfectly reasonable answer is, 'It's my calling.' We shouldn't lose sight of this – MSE is without doubt a calling and one that is often experienced powerfully. Another equally valid answer to the challenge is, 'If I wasn't ordained we wouldn't be having this conversation.' The MSE is present because the Church authorizes clergy as its representatives in the working world.

How are MSEs made? Most MSEs and SSMs train for ordination on a part-time basis on a regional course. When ordained, they undertake a curacy, normally over three years. This training follows a very similar pattern to paid curates. Subsequently they often remain in the same parish, giving what time they can to church ministry. Most MSEs (for reasons outlined below) are, technically, licensed as SSMs.

MSE employer agreements

Current and potential MSEs face a huge institutional barrier at the present time. The Church of England currently seeks a written agreement, signed by a senior employer representative, signalling consent to the MSE's ministerial involvement at work. The intention is that the minister's role is authorized and defined by both church and employer. Organizations are, however, reluctant to commit to such a document. After all, in employment terms, nothing has changed – the MSE does not expect time off for workplace ministry or a change of duties. The real sticking point is diversity – employers cannot be seen to favour one faith over others. Expecting an employer, whether in the public or private sector, to explicitly recognize and authorize MSEs is now deeply unrealistic. Employer agreements are, today, virtually non-existent – yet bishops' advisory panels insist on them for potential MSEs.

This needs urgent attention. Current policy means in fact that high-potential MSEs have only one option – to present as conventional SSMs. As a result, selection questions focus on associate parish ministry. These candidates have little opportunity to reflect on what it might mean to be ordained in their place of work (and probably won't be asked about work as a calling). As things stand there are few officially designated MSEs in training, even though in practice this is the ministry many will exercise (largely unacknowledged) after ordination.

This is not to say that employer *understanding* isn't important and helpful. MSE relationships with employers are built informally, through relationships of trust. Stories abound of careful negotiation and explanation, which is in itself a ministry. These conversations are vital, allowing work organizations to interact with the Church and its representatives in ways that would not happen under other circumstances. Discussions usually lead to something more than mere consent; senior managers not only come to understand MSEs but also become active supporters – in the good seats at their ordination. The lack of formal documentation in fact increases the depth of trust required and the need for sensitive explanations of what it means to be ordained and at work. For MSEs where evidence is required this will almost certainly be a supportive letter or occupational reference that reflects verbal agreement. The strict requirement of formal employer agreements disables ministry in secular employment.

Also important is to think about what is said about MSEs at the point of ordination. At present, normally the workplace is only mentioned where a written employer agreement is available, so it happens rarely. As a result, at ordination only the title parish is announced. For MSEs who clearly (and realistically) have work as their main focus, a positive step forward would be to acknowledge this less formally – 'licensed to X, but working as MSE in Y'. If it's impractical or undiplomatic to name a specific employer, there seems no reason why a sector or profession can't be named instead.

A more generous theology of work

MSE connects work and church, and it's important to reflect on what that means. The Church acknowledges that it is not reaching people between the ages of 20 and 50. One of the biggest factors is work. Work absorbs more of our time and energy than it has done for many previous generations. Church attendance has declined at the same time that work insecurity has increased. This isn't just an issue of Sunday working or the 24/7 economy. Many workers are expected to be in work, or focused on it, most days of the week. We take work home or go into the office at weekends. Many struggle with long working hours or zero hours contracts. If the Church is failing to reach a generation, it's because they are earning a living. When reaching busy people is difficult, reaching them at work makes a lot of sense.

The Christian tradition is ambivalent about work, seeing it as both a curse and a blessing. After Eden, humans have had to work to survive and physical labour is associated with pain. Other traditions affirm work as a blessing, a gift, even a form of spirituality. The Rule of St Benedict famously elevated simple manual tasks into a form of worship. Within the Protestant work ethic hard work was seen as a duty, an appropriate response to Providence.

Is God in our work? Twenty-first-century Christian sensibility remains uncertain. Listen for when jobs are mentioned in intercessions. There is an accepted pecking order: bishops, then clergy, then Readers and lay church workers, then, if time permits, one or two other jobs in a narrow band get a mention. We pray for doctors, nurses and teachers – jobs with a kind of quasi-religious status. When did you last hear a prayer for chartered accountants? This may well reveal an underlying half-suspicion that most work is fairly grubby and God wouldn't touch it with a bargepole. Rod Hacking goes to the heart of the matter:

> Industry and commerce do of course feel as if they embody values which are far distant from those of the Christian faith and I do not underestimate the struggles of those who seek to serve just one God within them. I equally understand why many Christians look on their work as some kind of necessary evil as the church is the embodiment of what is most good, to which they might well wish to give of themselves to a considerable degree. But neither can I avoid the feeling that such ambivalence towards the world of work is ultimately rooted in a mistaken, or inadequate, understanding of God and his purposes in creation as well as an inadequate understanding of how the church stands in relation to them.
>
> (Hacking, 1990, p. 59)

Work is not something 'other', or separately 'out there', as Chapter 6 argues. Where work causes us to ask questions, it is central to human existence: 'All work worthy of being called spiritual and worthy of being called human is in some way prophetic . . . Such work is, in a real sense, God's work' (Fox, 1995, p. 13).

Others point to the way congregations need support to be Christians at work – Armand Larive, in *After Sunday*, recounts the testimony of a sales manager who felt his Lutheran church required him to be a 'little Christ' to colleagues at work, but offered little advice in how this might happen (Larive, 2006, p. 64).

Through their work, MSEs celebrate the presence of God in all human activity. They point to the values that underlie work and tell the Christian story in a very particular language and context. Sometimes they help colleagues to integrate faith and life. Most of the time, they do their paid job to the best of their ability. MSEs undertake an important if often invisible aspect of mission by affirming God's concern for every part of creation. As Alan Ecclestone writes:

> All of life is spiritual, for all is part of God's creation. There is no division between sacred and secular, work and worship, religion and politics. Spirituality is not apart from our daily life; it is our daily lives. But it is a life with a cutting edge not avoiding the pain and fear.
>
> (Ecclestone et al., 1986, p. 1)

This is where MSEs work, where they are, bidden or not bidden. MSE remains a ministry with considerable potential. This might be a good time to rediscover it.

MSE in practice

Rob Fox, MSE, Newcastle Diocese, CHRISM Committee Member since 1995, customer relationship manager at HM Revenue and Customs

How and why I became an MSE

I describe myself as an MSE and have always done so. When I was ordained in 1991, I believed I was pointed to NSM ministry, although I resisted the idea of being a non-stipendiary 'clone' of a parish priest. During the 1970s I met an MSE based in an Anglican church and also teaching at

Manchester University – a really influential role model. Partway through training I was pointed in the direction of Stan Frost, the standard bearer for worker priests and industrial mission in the north-west – another inspiring individual.

My experience of MSE

I was placed as a curate initially in Stalybridge and then in Ashton-under-Lyne. I worked with two training incumbents who fortunately were both interested in MSE and happy to allow me flexibility to explore options. I covered all the bases in terms of parish-based training, but there was little formal recognition of what I was doing in the workplace. However, enough people in the diocese understood what I was doing and I became an informal adviser on MSE matters. Everyone, including the bishops, was supportive and I had a good relationship with DDOs as well – I undertook a lot of vocations work with people called to this ministry. Nothing was recognized formally, but I know I encouraged a number of new MSEs.

I continue to be informed and inspired by CHRISM. In 1984 there was a conference of 130 non-stipendiary ministers who debated whether their primary focus was work or parish. There was a 50/50 split and the organization Christians in Secular Employment Trust (CHRISET) was formed to support workplace ministry. CHRISM was developed in 1993 as an operational arm. It publishes the magazine *Ministers-at-Work* and every year runs a conference and a weekend retreat for MSEs.

What's the main focus of my ministry?

I've been with HMRC since I was 28 and that's where I have always worked as an MSE. My colleagues were hugely supportive all through training and have been ever since. I've never had a formal employer working agreement – it wouldn't be appropriate to ask. What I've had is much better – support, affirmation, encouragement, trust.

I currently work in HMRC's Large Business Directorate. Since 1986 I've also been involved in training and development in various capacities. Although I've worked in huge offices, mostly I've worked in communities of around 100–120 people and I work with wider 'virtual' communities too. They quickly get to know I'm ordained. In learning and development work it's vital to build on people's strengths. To help them learn, I start by letting them know who I am and how I learn. Often I talk about my training to be a priest. That opens doors immediately. I don't believe in '15-minute God-slots' in the workplace and they're fairly unpopular! I work towards an expression of faith which is seamless, integrated, natural.

Support and training

I trained on the Northern Ordination Course and, although little on the course was focused on workplace ministry, the Principal was sympathetic to the idea, which was a good thing as nearly everyone being ordained was in full-time work. One part of the course that was really helpful was contextual theology and, of course, I still use it.

I can't say I've been offered much training in workplace ministry. My last diocese ran some relevant courses, but if you work full time, even sessions run in the evening can be impossible to get to. MDRs have been interesting – reviewers seemed very tentative about what to ask and I've had to prompt with appropriate questions, but I know that's true for all MSEs being reviewed by people with little experience of workplace ministry.

Challenges and difficulties

Workplace ministry requires a delicate touch – HMRC has a requirement that all religious activities at work are registered, to ensure diversity and to prevent people being offended. However, you can't register every pastoral conversation! I've only just arrived in my new office and already people have begun interesting conversations. Much is deeply personal – and people welcome absolute confidentiality. Some of the time people want to know what the Church thinks about a particular issue. It's a fantastic opportunity to help people understand what the gospel is really about.

Most difficulties encountered by MSEs come from the Church; even if it's sympathetic it only has a 'head' not a 'heart' understanding of workplace ministry. Colleagues in chapter lose interest if you're not talking about parish life. In recent years I've seen a distinct shift of focus on to the parish, no doubt prompted by the perceived 'cliff edge' of 2025 when a large number of stipendiary clergy will have retired. The consequences are huge: the average age of those being ordained by the C of E has gone up from 43 to 52 – which means that the working life of trained clergy is now much shorter. It's a crisis that seems to be paralysing parishes and prevents any real interest in reaching people in the workplace. Most dioceses pulled out of industrial mission projects years ago.

The best thing about MSE

The people! Affirmation from work colleagues makes a huge difference. Being ordained in the workplace really does make a difference. I once had an extended posting to Jersey and an introductory email to staff from the boss told them I was a 'vicar'. Word got around instantly. People were really interested in what an ordained person was doing working for HMRC. Soon I was writing a column in the *Jersey Evening Post*, where my MSE role was mentioned, and regularly speaking at business and church events. We ran a lunchtime forum in St Helier where people from the financial community came to discuss all kinds of issues.

A supportive church environment helps, too. In my experience, MSEs need a community of faith as a base – it keeps them grounded but also allows them to help congregations to look outward and enables them to make sense of their communities, their social lives and their work.

Looking forward

Having moved to a new area, transferring to a new work context has been straightforward. It's less so moving diocese – SSMs/MSEs don't experience a handover process. An introduction from my last diocese plus a short note of my experience would have made a big difference. SSMs have to make contacts themselves and sound out where a local incumbent might take them on. It's an odd system. Where experienced SSMs move on you'd think the Church would want to engage them quickly and systematically, finding a good fit.

I look forward to continuing as a workplace minister. People know who I am; they know my story, so they come to talk to me. It's where I belong.

9

Making it work

This chapter explores how SSM works in practice, looking at licensing, working relationships and working agreements. We will examine some typical headings in a working agreement and spot some of the areas of difficulty, as well as looking at practical strategies for making the document more useful.

Licensing

Most SSMs in the Church of England are licensed by their diocesan bishop, giving the minister permission and authority to work in a defined context. Even where the minister has distinct commitments outside the Church, a licence is nearly always to a particular parish or benefice.

What difference does it make to be serving under a licence? This question is often asked by SSMs, particularly those approaching retirement, or those who have little time to offer in parish ministry. The alternative is to hope that a bishop will grant permission to officiate (PTO) status. Most PTOs are retired clergy. PTOs can sometimes claim fees as well as expenses for funerals and weddings, but licensed clergy often can't (practice varies widely – check your diocese's policy when drawing up your working agreement).

Holding a licence means that the Church expects something of you – duties defined in a working agreement. A licensing service is a public statement, showing that you are attached to a worshipping community, authorized with a clear role title, expected to be given duties, but also expected to make a measurable contribution. It means you're visible. A bishop has 'placed' you into a specific context, usually in a public act of worship. The congregation know you've arrived and you have a part to play. Being licensed usually means that you become a voting member of the PCC. It also means you're visible to the diocese – licensed SSMs should be on clergy mailing lists and invited to learning events, clergy conferences and to chapter and deanery meetings. Licensing also means you serve under Common

Tenure – standard terms covering issues like appointment, resignation, retirement and disciplinary procedures. If you are licensed to another role, such as an officer role within the diocese, this might happen in a less formal setting such as a committee meeting.

Working relationships[1]

The 'Calling far and wide project' researched job satisfaction among 'assistant ministers' and noted:

> Several interviewees indicated that the experience of assistant ministry could be highly influenced by the nature of the relationship with the incumbent. A positive relationship seemed to be accompanied by a good level of communication, autonomy and support for the assistant minister; less positive relationships seemed to be based more on direct delegation and often a lack of recognition, and could lead to some problematic outcomes.
>
> (Church of England Ministry Division, 2017, p. 7)

A congenial and professional relationship between incumbent and SSM is central. It's the relationship that matters most. A well-drafted working agreement is a starting point, especially if it begins with an honest discussion. However, even with the best of intentions, working relationships sometimes experience problems. Clergy have only limited training and experience of working in teams and for some it doesn't come naturally. Some incumbents find it hard to share information and delegate, just as some SSMs can be intransigent. Rather than focusing on duties, begin with expectations, being clear about what each person expects and hopes for. Then add a healthy dose of realism – what is likely to work in practice?

Most working agreements include a clause outlining steps to be taken if things are not working. Whatever on paper is the last, formal resort, colleagues need to find ways of dealing with differences of opinion and everyday sources of friction. Depersonalize situations by talking about outcomes rather than working style. Check carefully in advance if you are about to do or say something which treads on a colleague's toes (assume that it will). If you have something difficult to say, don't put it in writing; say it one to one in private, once your initial emotional response has quietened. If you're questioning the letter rather than the spirit of a working agreement, something has already gone wrong. If you have to kick the issue upstairs to the archdeacon or bishop, that probably means the problem is too difficult to patch over. Keep having civilized discussions, agree to disagree and plan a way forward.[2]

Supporting colleagues

In July 2017, in a General Synod discussion on clergy well-being, Justin Welby said: 'The hardest work I have ever done, and the most stressful, was as a parish priest. It was isolated, insatiably demanding, and I was, on the whole, working without colleagues. That wears people down.'

SSMs fulfil a vital role when they actively support colleagues – especially incumbents. Where relationships of deep trust develop, the rewards on both sides are immense. It helps if your colleague is prepared to disclose areas of vulnerability, but in any working relationship involving SSMs, loyalty is an absolute. It's as important a part of clergy discipline as prayer and study. Being loyal doesn't mean blind compliance, but it does mean that you debate matters behind closed doors. Every SSM has an important responsibility to support and respect colleagues – especially an incumbent besieged on all sides. Support is measured by outcomes, not empty promises. So if a member of the congregation criticizes the vicar in your presence, the only safe answer (excepting unsafe or illegal practice) is: 'You need to raise that with the vicar directly.' Becoming the figurehead for a lobbying group can be highly seductive, but very divisive.

Supervision

'Supervision' may seem an odd term here, but technically, incumbents are responsible for managing SSMs. Supervision will be much lighter than curate training and should feel rather more like peer review. Legally, your work is an extension of the work of an incumbent and what you do reflects on the person in charge. If you make a serious error of judgement or fail to follow important procedures, the incumbent will take some or all of the blame.

Supervision in most contexts is more a matter of mutual support between colleagues, but useful coaching questions can be asked, sometimes looking at accountability in straightforward terms. If your working agreement includes specific goals (the kind of language that seems to feature increasingly in a ministry development review (MDR)), you will undoubtedly be asked if you've met them.

Accountability

Accountability is an interesting topic for SSMs. Ultimately, as the Ordinal reminds us, accountability is to a higher power and then, of course, to a bishop. In practice, accountability for clergy is a work in progress. When Common Tenure was introduced in 2011 as an updated means of systematically recording the rights and duties of clergy, it was widely believed that this would allow dioceses to have more robust conversations with clergy deemed to be underperforming. It has allowed the Church to set clearer boundaries in terms of fixed-term appointments and retirement age, but to date there is little evidence that the measure is effective in addressing competency or performance issues (to borrow business language).

Clergy are responsible for a wide range of activities, record keeping, standards and legal duties. Associate ministers, paid or unpaid, have few targets of this kind to achieve, although pressures can arise when a vacancy occurs. Generally they are expected to meet parochial need as far as their time allows. There is an expectation that this time will be predicted in a working agreement. One advantage of such agreements is that they avoid the problem of wildly unrealistic expectations.

In practice, accountability boils down to the relationship between the SSM and the incumbent – effectively the SSM's line manager. An incumbent must agree before the SSM can be licensed. A newly arrived incumbent may choose not to use licensed SSMs already in place. Incumbents have only partial control over some parish decisions (style of worship, for example), but absolute control over how and when other ministers are used. Even though you are licensed, there is no statutory requirement for an incumbent to offer you something to do. Sadly, in some instances this mean that skilled SSMs are used less than they should be. In theory, senior clergy may be approached if SSMs feel their working agreements are being ignored, but in practice this is a remedy of last resort and the problem may remain unsolved. If an incumbent doesn't want to use the SSM or wants to limit his or her ministry, at present there is little that the institution can do about it. This underlines the importance of meaningful conversations about written agreements and good working relationships, but points to an important structural problem – everything depends on decisions made by incumbents. In the long term, SSM licensing may need be rethought completely, so their workload does not depend so heavily on the goodwill and imagination of local stipendiary clergy.

Time given to ministry

Associate ministers moving into new posts often approach them with mixed feelings. Initial conversations about commitment will probably feature a heady mix of optimism and guilt. Naturally you feel optimistic about what you bring to the role and the amount of time you will be able to commit. The new context will probably be busy; therefore you need to hit the ground running. The simple questions, 'What can you offer?' or 'What would you like me to do?' are more problematic than they appear.

SSMs vary in the amount of time they can give to parish work, but (as Chapter 4 reports) the average SSM gives around 30 hours a week. Even those in full-time jobs often give more than 20 hours a week in parish work (see Morgan, 2011, p. 15). Many are overstretched. One difficulty is that their availability may change on a week-by-week basis, risking frustration to diaries and rotas. Colleagues, churchwardens and senior clergy can make uninformed and unhelpful assumptions about SSMs' working hours. Expectations are often very local. For example, if a previous SSM had little availability, the same may be assumed about you. Equally, if the parish has experience of SSMs who have effectively been full-time clergy, you may present surprising constraints.

When thinking about the hours you propose to give to church work, bear in mind that you will almost certainly predict things inaccurately at first. New ministers often underestimate the amount of time relatively ordinary duties take, especially service preparation. More experienced clergy quickly learn to aim for 'good enough' rather than perfection. Even so, a minister's working week will often be reshaped by what Harold Macmillan may have wearily described as 'events, dear boy, events'. The average minister's workload is predictably unpredictable. If such disruption is routine, it can become exhausting. At the same time, there will be the usual mix of miscommunication, fallings out and other forms of emotional mayhem that can easily feature in parish life. For SSMs the added factor is that disturbances might arise from events that have nothing to do with church. A work crisis can put so much extra pressure on the SSM that parish responsibilities have to be put on hold temporarily. Planning for such crises is an important part of many SSMs' working agreements.

Here again, it's important to keep asking questions about the focus of ministry. One guide for curates suggests:

> There is no single model for non-stipendiary ministry. Much will depend on the home circumstances and/or the employment responsibilities of the individual. An important question to consider from the time of discernment and throughout training is how the focus of your future ministry will be identified. A parish-focused NSM sees the context of ministry in much the same way as his stipendiary colleagues; a work-focused NSM sees the sphere of her ministry predominantly in terms of her workplace and wider professional networks.
>
> (Witcombe, 2012, p. 16)

Unlike conventional work situations, it's meaningless to ask the question, 'How much work is there to do?' The experience of ministry is that there is always far more work to be done than time available. Justin Lewis-Anthony records a comment made on a clergy retreat – 'Even if I clear all the paperwork from my desk, there are still 5,000 people out there who need visiting' – and concludes that parish ministry 'by definition, is impossible to complete' (Lewis-Anthony, 2009, pp. 50 and 59).

Work overload has been a feature of life for clergy for many decades and recent studies point interestingly to 'emotional labour' – service industry work requiring a permanent smile, patience and sometimes near-constant availability. Statistically this kind of work is more often performed by women than men – for example, in the hospitality industry. In plain terms, the effort of generally 'being nice' is activity that drains. The impact of the unboundaried 'emotional labour' undertaken by clergy was touched on in a recent study. This identified that for clergy, 'withdrawing emotional labour is not an available choice'; ordained ministers are a 'distinctive example of emotional labour precisely because work and life are uniquely embraced by ordination. Unlike commercial airline workers, 21st-century clergy find it less easy to subtract who they really are from the ordained parts' (Peyton and Gatrell, 2013, pp. 120–1).

The same study noted, looking at clergy appointments, that '70 per cent of paid part-time posts are thought to be occupied by women . . . and the number of non-stipendiary clergy over half of whom are female continues to increase' (Peyton and Gatrell, 2013, p. 19). The pressures faced by SSMs and those working in part-time stipendiary roles are therefore not gender neutral. It will be interesting to see more work in this area, particularly when studies include SSMs.

Working agreements

A template for a working agreement is provided in the Appendix to this book. A working agreement is not technically part of a licence, but it is expected that you will agree one promptly. They're not to be confused with learning agreements – required for all curates in training. Learning agreements are detailed documents listing not just duties but learning objectives. Working agreements come for the next stage of ministry, when the SSM becomes an associate minister.

Working agreements for SSMs vary enormously. There was a time when the very concept of clergy defining and documenting their working arrangements seemed alien. Working agreements are sometimes referred to with a wry smile and some clergy are reluctant to take them seriously. If producing one is simply a form-filling exercise, an important opportunity has been wasted. A working agreement is a form of contract. This might sound like surprising language for unpaid work. It may not include the rights and obligations found in a contract of employment, but has strong parallels with the written terms issued to volunteers in other organizations. However, the comparison is not perfect, because the commitment of SSMs is so broad – the undocumented assumption is that you will do what you can, where you can, until you retire. It is a way of setting boundaries around a complex work relationship. If your colleague hasn't worked with SSMs before, much of Chapter 7 will assist in explaining SSM from first principles.

Too often, working agreements are agreed with minimal discussion, filed and never see the light of day again. All working agreements should include a review date. A new agreement should be reviewed after no more than six months, when you will have a clearer sense of what expectations mean in practice and how things are going. Refreshing the document doesn't need to be time-consuming or difficult and tends to mean checking whether you're doing the things you offered to do. Knowing why hopes have not been fulfilled is helpful. Subsequently it should probably be reviewed every two years or so. The usual reason for review is change – changes in circumstances and changes in you. Remember that growth doesn't always happen on its own; it's a good idea to allocate some time every year to explore new tasks and new ways of working (see Chapter 10 for more on personal development).

Before starting to draft a document, have at least one exploratory conversation – see the introductory material to the sample working agreement at the back of this book. What your working agreement says in print is less important than the relationship and the conversation that frames it.

When you begin drafting, be clear which parties are involved. A curate in training has relationships of accountability with a training incumbent and with a director of ministry training. An associate minister will be known to the church hierarchy, but usually has one key working relationship – with the incumbent. As discussed, local incumbents have huge leeway about the way they use licensed SSMs – or otherwise. If this working relationship is not defined honestly, realistically and flexibly, difficulties lie ahead.

Pressures on MSEs

MSE offers challenges to working arrangements. It is less well known than conventional SSM work, which means that those responsible for selecting, training, deploying and supporting clergy are not always familiar with the needs of MSEs. It is still relatively rare to find teaching about MSEs within ordination training or continuing professional development programmes.

Well-informed training incumbents support MSEs in developing the whole of their ministry, both at work and in church. However, in many cases MSEs have to define their own ministerial practice and negotiate the training and support they need on an individual basis. MSEs can experience the pressures of what is effectively a 'portfolio' life – attempting to balance family, work and church commitments. This calling is not for those who are reluctant to ask for help or individuals who expect every step of the path to be clearly defined. MSEs need to be flexible in their interaction with church, proactive in seeking development opportunities, robust in setting working boundaries and creative in their ability to explain what they do.

MSEs can sometimes feel invisible – their working commitments mean that they are unable to participate in parish life during working hours and hardly ever available for diocesan events or clergy chapter meetings. They may feel isolated in the work they do, potentially unrecognized by both church and workplace. Some report that the Church can sound frustrated about their lack of availability for parish activities and show little interest in anything else they do. During the MDR process, it seems that only enlightened reviewers appreciate that all of the MSEs' life is ministry, not just the time they spend in the parish. Only a minority ask appropriate questions about the full range of MSEs' work. Chapter 10 offers some remedies.

SSM in practice

Mike Kirby, SSM priest-vicar, Chester Cathedral, university lecturer

How and why I became an SSM

I spent 22 years in the health service and always thought that was my vocation. Starting at the Christie Hospital in Manchester in 1988 and later at the Royal Preston Hospital, I have served as a radiotherapy physicist and eventually as a consultant, at both institutions. During my scientific career, I gradually discovered that I had a calling to fulfil my own self, to be the calling Rowan Williams describes as 'called by God to be distinctly themselves, to exist as themselves'.

My experience of SSM

I was ordained deacon in 2013 and after serving as a curate in Blackburn Cathedral I was licensed to my current role at Chester Cathedral in December 2013. SSM priest-vicar is an interesting role. I undertake a wide range of duties, although I am only available to conduct services on Friday, Saturday and Sundays. I also work two days a week as a lecturer at Liverpool University and one day a week as hospital chaplain at the Countess of Chester Hospital. It makes for a full week, knowing that none of the roles can be restricted to just the days mentioned!

What's the main focus of my ministry?

My work still focuses on cancer therapy, but in a teaching capacity – I work as a lecturer in medical physics at Liverpool University. I continue to see teaching as an important part of my vocation. I think I'm in a very unusual position as a science lecturer. I wear my clerical collar at work, with the full consent of my university, and although I am teaching science rather than discussing my role as a minister, naturally it leads to questions outside the lecture theatre. Interestingly, some students ask, 'What's that round your neck?' – which perhaps shows how much of a gulf exists between church and society today. Of course, there are huge questions about the interface between faith and science, and working in a university provides opportunities for fascinating discussions, as long as I continue to recognize that the goodness of God is revealed in many different ways and the Christian perspective is not a monopoly. This teaching role is a big focus of my ministry – I consider myself to be a scientist and a priest and a teacher, very much a 'public Christian'. People don't come to church, so we need to find them.

Support and training

I trained full time at Westcott House in Cambridge, an unusual route for a potential SSM. The course was an excellent preparation, but it concerns me that a training course largely for stipendiary clergy said barely anything at all about SSMs or working alongside volunteers in general. It seems such an important aspect of ministry that I struggle to understand why it's not mentioned in training. I served as an SSM curate in Blackburn Diocese while also lecturing four days a week. I would reflect that we probably don't give SSM curates enough opportunities to anticipate the pressures, stresses and opportunities of this particular ministry. We need to see the value and worth in all types of ministry: stipendiary and non-stipendiary, full time and part time.

Challenges and difficulties

It's sometimes difficult to adjust mentally to the rapid changes of context in my work, moving from hospital to church to university. There is often a regular pattern to what I do, which can lead to work stress. I find it's really important to utilize my downtime creatively and effectively. I have support networks in place, but also recognize that exhaustion is a factor.

The best thing about SSM

I think SSM is a *vital* ministry. It's community focused and possibly the closest thing we have to Jesus' Galilean ministry – being among people, where we find them and answering questions in communities where most people don't go to church. It demonstrates that ministry can be real, worthwhile, important and connected with living the path. In a society where weekends really don't mean anything any more, we really are going to have to reach out to people in the place where they work and study; and when they do it.

Looking forward

I'm thoroughly open to ideas for development and I'm a natural resource finder. As an SSM you have to be – you can't wait for opportunities to be floated in your direction. But the fruits of God's work are always out there, in so many different ways – especially outside the church buildings. Perhaps within the institutional Church, we need to be more open to seeing what opportunities SSMs can bring, for being disciples anywhere and everywhere.

10

Developing your ministry

This chapter suggests ways you might review and develop as an SSM.

Staying motivated

The 'Experiences of ministry' project aims to discover what helps clergy remain effective ministers. In 2017, the survey focused on the experiences of SSMs, with 94 per cent agreeing with the statement, 'My sense of call is as strong as it was when I was first ordained' (Church of England Ministry Division, 2017, p. 4). The summary noted that many SSMs 'frequently experience positive mood and low exhaustion at the end of a day'.

The term 'engagement' is in vogue among human resources specialists – how far staff feel positively committed to their work. Occupational psychologists tell us that we are motivated by a range of factors. Daniel Pink's book *Drive* (2011) points out the power of meaningful work, suggesting that key factors are autonomy (having some control how you perform a task), mastery (your skills and knowledge keep improving) and purpose (you contribute purposefully to your colleagues, customers or to society).

Clergy, like everyone in work, get more out of their roles when they become aware of what motivates them. 'Experiences of Ministry' analysed the time that SSMs spend on different activities. Unsurprisingly, most time is spent on the predictable: liturgical duties, administration, travelling, preaching and teaching. Respondents spent on average less than half an hour a week on a range of things that might potentially be stimulating, including 'leadership in local community', activities outside the parish, planned outreach, children and youth work, running nurture courses, plus finding more time for professional development. Stipendiary clergy also reported wanting to spend more time doing some of the same things.

Ideas for development

What can you do to expand your ministry? Here are some suggested ideas for exploration.

- **Wear a different hat** try on a role you haven't done before, such as chairing a PCC, leading a study group, giving a talk about your working life.
- **Exchange roles** for a fixed, brief period, swap duties with a colleague working in the same team.
- **Lead a project** create an opportunity to lead a specific area of work.
- **Stretch your comfort zone** find a chance to do something you've never done before. Rural ministry? Youth work? Entertaining pre-schoolers? Leading a theological reflection?
- **Seek increased responsibility** take on increased responsibility in one or two areas.
- **Initiate a workplace project** if you're an MSE, try out new ideas in your place of work.
- **Shadowing** shadow (or at least talk to) someone doing an interesting role.
- **Learn about something different** study a topic you know nothing about.
- **Take a break** negotiate time off (even if it's just a long weekend) to reflect, think and recharge your batteries.

Working with boundaries

A criticism aired about SSMs is that they 'cherry-pick' their tasks – avoiding administration, perhaps, or having limited availability for midweek services. *How* you indicate non-availability is a vital skill, otherwise you reinforce prejudices. Avoid any sentence starting with, 'Because I'm an SSM, I don't . . .'. All ministry is about boundaried – but generous – availability. Do what you can, when you can and try to vary your availability. For example, if a colleague is on summer leave you might make yourself free for some midweek commitments. Besides, working off a limited menu is likely to keep you too securely in your comfort zone, stifling personal development. It's positive to take on unfamiliar tasks and slightly risky – especially the things people don't expect you to do. So, for example, if your time commitments mean you need to focus on worship and have little time for committee meetings, it might be helpful to reverse that balance over a fixed period.

Associate leadership

When do SSMs take on a leadership role? The most likely context will be a vacancy or, potentially, in an interim post. Otherwise, SSMs still occupy an important leadership role, described in the title of a current CPAS programme and elsewhere as 'leading from the second chair'. This role is nuanced, complex and often very rewarding.

Associate leadership means taking a number two (or sometimes number three) position, supporting and advising around key decisions. It's a role where affirmation and loyalty matter. Loyalty isn't about subservience or blindly following instructions, but exercising a sensitive form of leadership. For example, how do you exercise leadership when an incumbent makes unpopular decisions or offends key members of the congregation? How do you fill the 'second chair' unobtrusively when you have more experience of work and ministry? When your incumbent is significantly younger than you or less confident? How do you lead with integrity where there are real differences of opinion or working style? Where no one acknowledges that you have a leadership role at all?

These questions are relatively new to the Church and they arise now because SSMs are doing more, increasingly taking up leadership functions even if not visibly in leadership roles. In the past, bishops' advisory panels (BAPs) have made a clear distinction between those with sufficient leadership ability to be incumbents and those with rather more limited leadership skills who are selected as assistant ministers. This either/or thinking is increasingly disconnected from what's happening on the ground. Additionally, leadership programmes are principally designed for stipendiary clergy. This makes sense on one level, but we can do a great deal more to recognize and develop leadership skills in SSMs. This will be partly about providing the right experiences and partly about building on what they can already do. Where clergy are in short supply and expected to cover large areas, and as interim ministry develops, SSMs will increasingly be asked to be leaders.

How does an effective associate leader operate? The first require-ment is sensitivity – knowing how easy it is to tread on someone's toes or to become opposition rather than support. Communicate carefully and frequently – possibly more often than you think is strictly neces-sary (see Chapter 7). You will quickly learn whether your incumbent prefers this verbally or in a quick email. If in doubt, share information.

There are, of course, dangers. The first is interference – or any-thing that looks like interference. That's why you need to use careful language (not 'you really ought to' but 'you may not need to know this but I'm telling you because it might help avoid a problem'). Look hard at your motives – are you keeping colleagues in the loop, pro-moting a personal agenda or trying to look important? The second danger is oversupplying information. As a relationship of trust builds, you will learn from experience what colleagues need to be informed about immediately, what can wait and what can be dealt with quietly in the background. Otherwise you will find yourself beginning an uncomfortable sentence, 'I just assumed . . .'. Experience sets bound-aries better than principles – learn from each other so you recognize 'red flag' occasions and information and conversational minefields.

SSMs sometimes play the long-suffering card, 'Incumbents come and go and I pick up the pieces afterwards.' Hinting that you're a permanent feature is unhelpful and can easily make you an obs-tacle to change, particularly if you are vocally opposed to initiatives. Most experienced SSMs understand the pressures stipendiary clergy are under. When listening to a colleague preach you might think, 'I could do better,' but the real question is, 'Could I do the whole job, including the paperwork, the routine frustrations, plus the constant demands for pastoral attention, *and* still have energy to say anything meaningful on a Sunday morning?'

Characteristics of effective Christian leadership

Associate leadership shares many of the characteristics of mainstream church leadership as it is:

- **sensitive to context** adapting working methods to what is required in a particular place;
- **aware of its impact** knowing how the leadership style affects others;

- **inspired by a vision of what could be** motivated by growth and change;
- **setting clear goals** that a community shares;
- **honest about failure** open about what hasn't worked and what has been learned;
- **generous to other opinions** allowing space and time for contributions and feedback;
- **clear-minded enough to ensure decisions are made and acted on** not getting bogged down in reflection or repeated rounds of consultation;
- **enables ministry** of every kind in a context of shared learning and prayerfulness;
- **supported and encouraged** receiving support and constructive feedback from a range of sources, including colleagues.

Church leadership can be a frustrating or isolating task, but it can also be influential and effective, leading to communities that care about each other and care about being church. Associate leaders play an important part in building such communities, and have an important responsibility not to get in the way.

Trust is a key element in terms of building relationships and trust needs clear boundaries. For example, you need to know what decisions you can take alone, those you need to consult on and those decisions that have nothing to do with you. When you are covering for an incumbent who is on leave, discuss in advance issues that might come up and when you have authority to make a decision. Using example scenarios, talk about reasons why you might need to contact your colleague in an emergency (apply similar thinking to a colleague's day off). Boundaries, of course, have two sides – you should also be clear about when and why your time off might be interrupted.

Personal study and continuing professional development

Most clergy, in my experience, are hungry for learning. Sometimes this is about intellectual challenge, sometimes it is about personal development. Continuing learning matters to SSMs – the chance to grow (spiritually, in skill range, in insight, in experience) and the opportunity to experience new things.

At ordination, clergy faithfully promise to be diligent in their studies. Full-time stipendiary clergy sometimes struggle to find time for study, but they are encouraged to take study days and retreats, neither of which has to come out of their annual leave. In this respect stipendiary clergy have a clear advantage by working in a system that encourages and respects time out for development. Stipendiary clergy are paid for the days they spend studying, on retreat, attending conferences and taking a sabbatical. In contrast, for SSMs, days committed to study, professional development and spiritual growth are often taken from an annual leave allowance – therefore self-funded. Some SSMs lose income because they are not working. Churches spend considerable sums on continuing ministerial development (CMD), yet the need for accessible and relevant learning is frequently voiced by SSMs. Sara Scott, writing in *Diverse Gifts*, outlines the time pressures experienced: 'Priorities have to be assessed and the result is often a permanent feeling of guilt. Work and family have to take first place followed by church duties. Time for reading, reflection and spiritual refreshment is hard to find' (Torry, 2006, p. 57).

The 'Experiences of ministry' survey painted a relatively encouraging picture of SSMs being integrated into training and support structures, although a number of SSMs reported problems accessing learning events. Continuing ministerial development is generally open to SSMs, but many SSMs cannot attend sessions held during the working day. Some dioceses, according to Teresa Morgan, 'seem to decide at this point that SSMs do not fit their system, and effectively cease to offer them further development' (Morgan, 2011, p. 10).

One of the most pressing issues facing the Church is working out imaginative learning solutions for SSMs, especially those working full time. In fairness, it's difficult to deliver training to SSMs, who need wide-ranging content and have no shared view on the most convenient times and days for training events. Saturday courses seem to make sense, but a Saturday is often the SSM's day off. Some dioceses have experimented with courses on Sundays, which are sometimes popular with recipients. Others offer evening events beginning with supper, but this relies on convenient locations and short journey times after a working day. Access to learning for SSMs remains a key issue and there may be occasions when the Church needs to consider compensation for loss of earnings or for reducing someone's limited holiday allowance.

If SSM doesn't lead naturally to growth and change, a ministry review is essential. This, of course, should be more than a gentle 'How's it going?' conversation. SSMs need to be asked if they are still learning and how they could be stretched in the future.

Moving into a bigger role

Personal development isn't just about going on courses. Often it happens where someone is given the chance to work in a new role or at least take on new responsibilities. Some SSMs achieve this almost effortlessly – or that's how it seems. In reality, change of this kind may be initiated by the individual minister, not by the institution. Where SSMs are visible to senior clergy, at times they are encouraged to take on new roles or additional tasks. Some SSMs work as vocations advisers, for example.

While SSMs can attend courses, in general they are rarely offered new experiences, secondments or projects that are likely to encourage growth. Teresa Morgan's report asked SSMs how their ministry had developed:

> strikingly, 41% of respondents reported no change in their ministry since ordination. Only 14% have acquired extra responsibilities. Only 12.5% of the great majority in parish ministry have changed parish. 2.5% have fewer responsibilities now than when they were ordained (some due to personal circumstances; others because stipendiary colleagues have prevented them from exercising parts of their ministry) . . . One could view this as a praiseworthy picture of stability. In principle, it could be the result of a deliberate and carefully thought out policy by dioceses. Such a policy might make sense and would certainly have supporters, but I have not been able to discover that it exists. Meanwhile, the trend in recent years has been for stipendiaries to change post every few years. This, of course, is partly because most clergy have no longer had tenure and this pattern may change again with the introduction of Common Tenure. But the pattern of recent years has also been justified as good both for clergy and for those they serve. If it can be good for stipendiaries and their congregations to have a change every few years, the same could surely be said of non-stipendiaries.
>
> (Morgan, 2011, p. 12)

In terms of capacity to take on associate leadership roles, SSMs have important potential. They will only be available for such roles if they are given the right building blocks in terms of experience. Currently, evidence suggests that for many SSMs opportunities are not presented. Morgan argues a lack of policy:

> The current picture is not one of stability but of stagnation. Far too often, it seems, dioceses train ordinands – at considerable expense – ordain them and place them in a parish or chaplaincy, then simply forget about them. This surely cannot be the best use of resources at a time when the Church has so many projects and aspirations for mission and ministry, and never enough clergy to lead and help enact them.
>
> (Morgan, 2011, pp. 12–13)

Interim appointments

Recently the Church of England has followed other parts of the Anglican Communion (particularly the USA) by introducing interim ministry appointments.[1] Interim managers have been used in other sectors for at least half a century and offer considerable advantages in terms of analysing need, drawing resources together and offering plans for longer-term change. In principle such roles should allow SSMs with leadership experience opportunities to make a significant contribution. At present some congregations appear reluctant to accept interim ministers because it looks like a remedial measure or because it will make it harder to find a permanent incumbent in the future. Therefore it is uncertain how interim ministry will feature in practice and how much SSMs will be involved.

SSM in practice

Gina Radford, SSM curate, Deputy Chief Medical Officer, Whitehall

How and why I became an SSM

Having been an LLM for a few years, I felt a clear calling to be an ordained minister. At present, most of that ministry is in the workplace and outside the institutional setting of the Church. It took me a short while to reconcile the fact that I can spend relatively little time in the traditional parish-based ministry role and the need to manage my own and other people's expectations of me. I have come to a realization that I am called to minister wherever I am, which in reality is mostly in a secular environment and I'm very comfortable with that.

My experience of SSM

The reality of a ministry that might include life spent in secular work was not really touched on in any depth during my training. It feels as if none of my secular world experience or training counts. This seems to miss an important point. So many people in our congregations are struggling to live out their faith in the realities of the secular world of work, I wonder if we could do much more to meet them in conversation and understanding. I also think we are missing a huge opportunity in terms of supporting younger colleagues who may be called to the ministry before having had any extended period of working in secular employment. I suggest those of us who are daily facing the reality of inhabiting both the world of secular employment and ministry may have a lot to offer in terms of insight and experience for those who have not had this as a meaningful experience. I recently heard an incumbent bemoan the lack of willingness of certain people to attend midweek evening events. I have to put my hand up – I'm one of those people. When you have just done a long commute, had a day full of meetings and whatever else at work, you haven't had time to have supper, feed the cat or spend time with your family, it's hard to turn out again for an evening meeting. Similarly, finding time to read, pray and spend meaningful time with God can be very challenging – I often do Morning Prayer on the train, earphones in to cut out the distractions. My fellow commuters must wonder at this person mumbling away to herself, eyes closed – but little do they know that they are regularly in my prayers!

I am very fortunate in having a very supportive training incumbent and an employer who allows me to work from home one day a week. Another helpful factor has been knowing I am not the only one trying to juggle these different roles; there are three of us who trained together who offer each other support and share experiences.

What's the main focus of my ministry?

I have a strong sense of being a minister who is also in secular employment. I am not officially recognized as a workplace minister and I am very conscious that there are boundaries that I need to respect within my secular role. My witness and ministry within my secular employment is very much more about how I do my job rather than what I overtly say.

I am open about the fact I am ordained, but always take the lead from others as to how far I should go. I have had some amazing conversations with people about what I do and believe – but always at their instigation. My ministry is one trying to live out my witness in the day-to-day business of my secular role. Within my parish ministry I undertake as much as I realistically can in my limited time. I am conscious that opportunities for parish-based pastoral care are limited, as are opportunities to really enter into the life of the five villages I serve.

Support and training

I trained on the Eastern Regional Ministry Course. The training was standardized but included some electronic distance learning which worked very well. A lot of the training was contextually based and good preparation. However, I feel we could have spent more time looking at ministry in the secular world. I think that we could all benefit from much more discussion and exploration of what it means to live and minister or even sustain a faith in this context.

As far as curacy training is concerned, my experience so far is that it has felt very much like 'one size fits all'. It feels as if there is one path for training and that's it. Considering the range of ministers involved, that seems unrealistic. My diocese is trying to accommodate those of us in secular employment – holding additional evening IME sessions, for example. I and two colleagues recently raised the issue of sharing and exploring with our other curate colleagues what our experience of ministry is like, and we have been asked to put on a session on a future training day – that to me is a very positive step.

I have an amazing training incumbent – she is very realistic about what I can do, never pressures me or makes me feel guilty and is more protective than I am of my day off! She is a huge support and I know I am very fortunate to have her both as a fantastic role model, but also as a colleague.

Challenges and difficulties

Anyone working full time in a demanding job will find the demands of training exacting. There are clear expectations of what sessions you have to attend, but little recognition of the fact that someone like me has to take annual leave in order to commit to this training. This quickly eats away at your holiday allowance, reducing opportunities for rest and recovery.

Sometimes I feel guilty because I'm not offering my parishes more outside Friday to Sunday, but I would encourage every SSM to find a position where you are comfortable with your calling but still growing and experiencing as many opportunities as you can within the different facets of your ministry.

Also, it's really important to have a realistic working agreement. You need to be flexible but at the same time honest – with yourself and with your incumbent and parishioners. There are only so many hours in the day – and taking on too much is, as I am very much aware, the surest way to getting overwhelmed, exhausted and spiritually drained. Saying 'no' is one skill I am honing very effectively!

The best thing about SSM

I absolutely love it. It's a great privilege to meet people in this way. I'm enormously grateful that the Church of England recognizes people who want to make this kind of contribution and has the imagination to continue to bring people in from the secular world who are useful to the word of ministry. It's a great opportunity. Ministers in secular employment reflect the realities of modern life. They offer powerful insights, and are a bridge and a voice into the secular world. It's an important vision, but I don't think it's fully realized in the way people are trained or the way people and their experience and skills are used.

Looking forward

I'm continuing to enjoy and learn from the challenges of a ministry based in secular employment. It's an important, but often subtle, ministry. It's not immediately overt, but the wonderful thing is that I can get to places and have conversations that I couldn't do with a dog collar on or just by having 'Revd' in front of my name. I feel hugely blessed and enriched, having the opportunity to use my skills in such diverse ways. It's not a career trajectory I would ever have envisaged, but that's the wonderful thing about God's calling – it's rarely what we expect, but always more than we imagined!

11

The future shape of SSM

This chapter looks at the future of SSM and explores changes that are already happening. It includes a range of recommendations for rethinking how we deploy and support SSMs.

The decline in stipendiary clergy

The Church of England sees troubled waters ahead. Projections of declining, ageing congregations and falling income are major concerns, but so is the average age of clergy – in just over a decade there will be fewer stipendiary clergy available, even if there were funds to pay for them. Writing in the *Church Times* in 2014,[1] Linda Woodhead noted that 'traditional full-time stipendiary clergy are now the exception rather than the rule'. She argues that we have reached the 'end of a decade of respite for the Church of England – thanks to Anglicans offering to minister without pay. This is a decade in which the Church could have been planning for the predictable changes that are now in train.'

Woodhead offers a tough diagnosis, considering that many dioceses are thinking hard about future staffing. At the time of writing, several English dioceses are considering ways of grouping parishes together, pooling resources and staffing, to support churches that would not otherwise be able to afford clergy. The Diocese of Exeter has much to offer in terms of its experience. Exeter moved in 2003 to establish 'a dynamic grouping of smaller communities', coining the term 'mission communities'. It's a positive way of rethinking church, sometimes ecumenically, based on need and local resourcing. The model has much to commend it, but some way to go. It may ultimately prove to be a transition stage to even looser structures. Mission communities still rely heavily on stipendiary clergy, but provoke new thinking about lay leadership and ministry and the deployment of SSMs: 'The sharing of ministries is needed to enable the Church to express the fullness of its life locally' (Diocese of Exeter,

2003, p. 29). Other dioceses currently planning to adopt similar models may take the idea in new directions. Carlisle's scheme, launched in 2013, envisions communities led by a small number of stipendiary clergy, supported by SSMs, Readers and worship leaders working in pairs. This scheme also includes the United Reformed and Methodist churches.

Similarly, a 2014 Church in Wales ministry report announced a shift to 'ministry areas', with:

> a broad team of ministers in each ministry area, enabled by a team leader, who will be in priest's orders, and probably a stipendiary priest. However, we envisage that each ministry area will be served by several priests, although the greater number may well be non-stipendiary, complemented by other ministers and ministries.
>
> (Church in Wales, 2014, p. 8)

This built on a 2012 review that argued for the benefits of training more lay ministers and SSMs, adding, 'We believe that Non-stipendiary Ministry should receive greater encouragement in the Church in Wales than has sometimes been the case' (Church in Wales, 2012, p. 16).

The Scottish Episcopal Church faces considerable resource challenges. In 2011, its General Synod approved a 'Whole Church Mission and Ministry Policy' with 'a new focus on the support of clergy and on the development of partnership in ministry between clergy and laity'. The report argues:

> Congregations should strive to be world-facing communities, able to make connections with all who seek hospitality, community and a spiritual home. They should be overseen – singly or in clusters – by stipendiary clergy who have the capacity for strategic leadership and shared ministry.
>
> (Scottish Episcopal Church, 2011, p. 2)

The report refers to the difficulties of recruiting and funding stipendiary clergy, but does not offer solutions specifically focused on SSMs.

Other parts of the world have moved in similar directions and some have gone further. The Anglican Diocese of Auckland in New

Zealand has developed 'Local Shared Ministry', drawing on a model where clergy act as 'enablers' of much larger teams:

> All the members of the congregation, led by a Ministry Support Team, share the responsibilities that are traditionally carried by a vicar. Over the past two decades, in places where the trad-itional 'vicar-led' model was no longer sustainable, Local Shared Ministry has made it possible for Anglican ministry and mission to continue in those local areas.[2]

SSM or bi-vocational?

These developments reflect honest attempts to respect, maintain and also transform structures. Many denominations already blend paid and unpaid ministers, but the term 'bi-vocational' is now commonly in use in North America, with a wide range of interesting examples.[3] New ministers are offered a part-time salary and sometimes accom-modation, but there is a clear understanding that the minister will need alternative paid employment. Sometimes the community helps the minister find it.

Bi-vocational ministry has interesting possibilities. The role title affirms the idea that vocation and ministry exist outside the Church. The concept also brings challenges. SSMs encountering the idea often object to the implication that their vocation is split. Others see it as an all too easy way of maximizing clergy contribution at reduced costs. For some it provides clearer boundaries. Bi-vocational ministry is therefore a potential solution, striding the paid/unpaid fence.

Rosario Picardo writes about the experiences of the United Methodist Church in the USA where such a ministry has emerged, rooted in a sound theology of work:

> Across the board, church leaders will be faced with the chal-lenges of possibly working another job while engaged in ministry as a vocation, accepting a lower rate of pay for 'min-istry work', redefining worship/ministry space in more mod-est terms, and adjusting to a major cut in spending kingdom resources on excessive commodities that have been passed off as ministry necessities.

(Picardo, 2013, p. 89)

This hint of generous expenses seems unfamiliar this side of the Atlantic. Staffing pressures and economics may, however, make us look at bi-vocational ministry more closely in the future. At present, part-stipended roles appear to be more common. Changing circumstances may cause us to look at a fully fledged model of bi-vocational ministry and this may ultimately be the future for some forms of SSM. We have already seen the unplanned emergence of part-SSM roles. If we adopt bi-vocational ministry alongside conventional SSM, it would be better if this was the result of joined-up thinking rather than local invention.

Selecting SSMs and MSEs

As the Church of England comes to rely increasingly on SSMs, it may choose to rethink the way it selects them. Selection criteria could, for example, look in greater depth at the resilience required by prospective SSMs who will be working full time while also serving in a parish. Where the greatest change to thinking is required is around the role of associate clergy.

At present selectors look at two categories – candidates with the leadership potential to be incumbents and the rest. The assumption that only incumbents need fully developed leadership skills needs to be challenged. SSMs already have a growing role as associate leaders; many are already leaders in their workplaces. Ignoring this talent base is absurd. SSMs will need new skills to take on future interim roles or working in larger, more fluid teams. The development of what this book describes as a 'mixed economy' needs a more flexible approach to assessing potential. The model of 'father's little helper' outlined in one of the case studies is well out of date.

Tim Thornton, Bishop at Lambeth, published a blog in 2013 describing current policy around selection and training as a 'game of unreality':

> whether training to be stipendiary or self-supporting in the Church of England, in reality we have been shaping vicars. That is what we have understood ourselves to be doing and what the world, in turn, understands and expects us to provide. But, in what is a long overdue move, I believe it's essential for us to deconstruct the understanding or definition of a vicar. Instead

we need to reconstruct and permit new models of being deacons and priests so that they can be made 'real' and gain acceptance in the wider world. At present we all participate in a game of unreality. We go through a process of discernment of vocation which is for the order of deacon and priest but, in fact, everyone really knows we are trying to find people who can be leaders of our churches. We are looking for vicars . . . many dioceses are struggling to create and allow new ways of leading churches and ministering to fresh expressions of church – as well as to inherited models of church. Yet there is no clarity about models of ministry so that theological institutions are left in a dilemma about what they should be doing and how they can best shape and form people for the ministry that lies ahead.[4]

Linda Woodhead points to key difficulties: 'many of those who have been recruited and trained since the '80s are coming to ministry as a second or third career'.[5] She argues that SSMs' time in church ministry will be correspondingly shorter and the Church needs to find more ordinands, especially women, under the age of 35. Recent initiatives to attract younger clergy have been criticized as an over-optimistic attempt to return to a traditional model. Where the initiative has worked it has attracted men rather than women and, since its focus has been on identifying incumbents, has not generated younger SSMs. Indeed, the Church of England has yet to begin a conversation about how it might attract younger SSMs. To do so will pose questions – about how SSMs are seen by the Church, how they are trained and how they are deployed. The Church will probably need to promote SSM more widely, using a range of role models as examples. Demonstrating 'whole of life' ministry might encourage prospective ordinands to see SSM as a mid-career choice, not an end-of-career choice. Increased recognition of MSEs (and actively seeking them out once again) would reinforce this agenda enormously. More SSMs in their thirties and early forties would provide fresh perspectives to parish ministry and almost certainly greater length of service.

There is also a broader issue of gender, one that cannot be addressed in sufficient depth here. More women than men are SSMs – a reversal of the balance in stipendiary clergy. Within the Church, women tend to be in SSM or part-time posts and are under-represented in senior roles. Women who are part of a clergy couple are still sometimes unreasonably required to accept the role of SSM. There is a great deal more that needs to be explored and reflected on around the experience of female SSMs, particularly in relation to levels of responsibility and access to wider-ranging experience. Hopefully, current studies into clergy stress and emotional labour in stipendiary clergy will be extended to SSMs, with a particular focus on women's experience.

Revitalizing MSE

As Chapter 8 outlined, SSM was, in one sense, originally conceived as MSE. The Church anticipated ordaining clergy who continued to offer something to the world of work while supporting local parishes. We have lost sight of this original intention and of the role and value of MSEs. There are two main reasons we should revive this interest. First, mission – MSEs reach people in work and that's where people spend most of their waking time. The second reason is to increase numbers of both MSEs and SSMs. SSMs are at present slightly older on average than their stipendiary colleagues. We need younger SSMs and attracting them requires us to communicate the breadth of ministry encompassed, especially where it takes place outside the parish.

The Church needs to appreciate that formal employer agreements for MSEs are almost non-existent. Because this bar is set so high, some dioceses currently put forward few or no MSEs. Licensing of MSEs should draw on informal (but significant and carefully negotiated) recognition and support from employers. Every ordination and licensing of an MSE (or SSM with a strong focus on work) could make explicit reference to a place of work, a work sector or to a business community.

Deployment of SSMs

As the Church considers its future, much of its planning to date has been about asking stipendiary clergy to look after bigger and bigger units. There is hope that lay ministers will weigh in, but Reader numbers are declining. Some dioceses are thinking about ordaining more SSMs, but are not quite sure where they will be found. Linda Woodhead's article in the *Church Times*, quoted above, argues that changes to the structure of ministry have been 'gradual rather than planned', and this is an important insight. Besides, church leaders have not yet decided whether they can use the word 'deployment' in relation to SSMs. Assumptions about deployment of SSMs are out of date. We probably have better data now than any time in the past 50 years about where SSMs are and what they are doing. They have deployable skills and can perform a wider range of tasks. Current trends suggest that, in several dioceses, something like 50 per cent of licensed clergy will be SSMs. Any organization finding that half its professional workforce is unpaid needs to rethink the whole process – attraction, development, retention and deployment.

There are, in fact, signs that the Church is thinking about its diverse SSM cohort with more care and imagination – efforts to be valued considering the limited resources available. There is always more that can be done, but the focus needs to be on preparing SSMs for tasks on the near horizon. At present the Church is reinventing itself locally rather than through a national SSM strategy. It seems likely that policy will continue to be invented at ground-floor level. New variations are emerging all the time. SSMs are already leading parishes and benefices and holding important diocesan roles. Shortly we will no doubt see SSMs undertaking interim assignments – this one measure would have an enormous impact on SSMs' development and the way they are seen.

It makes no sense for some SSMs to be overstretched while others sit on their hands. A more uniform deployment of experience and talent may require centralized intervention. Where there is evidence of SSMs being sidelined or underused by incumbents, they should be licensed directly to a bishop or archdeacon. In the long term it might make sense for all SSMs to be licensed this way. Although it would add slightly to the workload of senior staff it would ensure that SSMs are called on in a way that matches their talent and experience.

This, of course, is not a one-sided conversation. If SSMs are to take on more interesting roles they have to be clear about their own flexibility and availability. They may be called on to take on new responsibilities at short notice, undertake short-term roles, develop greater associate leadership skills and sometimes commit to long-term periods of availability so they can be deployed with increased confidence. Even so, to be realistic, SSMs will need to continue to take much of the responsibility for their own professional development.

SSMs and vacancies

Chapter 10 outlined how taking on new responsibilities is one way that SSMs grow. For the average SSM this is most likely to happen in a vacancy. SSMs' experiences of vacancies have reportedly been mixed. Some SSMs have effectively been allowed, informally, to lead in the short term. Taking up the reins for a short period has enhanced the experience of many SSMs. Sometimes they have been invited into a different parish for the same purpose. There are signs that the Church might be considering short-term licensing in such circumstances. This would be a huge step forward. In the recent past, some SSMs have been excluded from decision-making during vacancies, effectively required to put their ministry on hold until the new incumbent arrives. In a few cases they have been quietly asked to move on when a new post-holder comes into place. Others have worked diligently to keep things afloat during more than one vacancy, without hearing from senior clergy during the process and with no 'thank you' when a new incumbent is in place.

What happens to SSMs during and after vacancies is a matter for urgent review. SSMs can often make their most significant contribution during a vacancy and enhance their skills at the same time. Experienced SSMs could be used more extensively to cover vacancies. There should be no circumstances where their ministry is ignored, taken for granted or – worse – suspended. Their future ministry needs to be discussed in depth as part of the appointment process.

Starting here

We will have to learn new techniques for managing SSMs. Sometimes this means caring for SSMs better or at least making more efforts to provide opportunities for development. Additionally, it makes sense to sound out SSMs about future deployment and to provide training and experience that will help them fill the gaps. This means increased attention to their training and development, preparing SSMs for the challenges of leading, and not just from the 'second chair'. As responsibilities increase, closer attention will need to be given to work–life balance and the risk of burnout.

Teresa Morgan is no doubt correct in suggesting, 'if non-stipendiary ministry did not exist today, we should probably be discussing whether to develop it' (Morgan, 2011, p. 29). It's interesting to speculate how

SSM might be designed if we were inventing it from scratch today. Would we make fudged compromises between economic need and a new vision of ordained ministry? Very possibly. We might be clearer about what SSM is *for* – transparent about the fact that we need SSMs in parishes, but also explicit about their wider value. We might learn to be interested once again in MSEs, not just tolerating their peculiarity but equipping them for mission. We need to reaffirm the meaning of the phrase 'self-supporting' – showing that it's not part-time ministry, but whole-of-life ministry, with work as an integrated feature. SSM matters and we can build on it. It is – in every sense of the phrase – a way of finding the kingdom at work.

SSM in practice

Biddi Kings, SSM, Worcester Diocese, manager of an online retail water plant nursery

How and why I became an SSM

I was ordained deacon in June 2003. As is the case for so many women entering ministry, my family circumstances are such that I am unable to consider relocating. For the Church of England, this is considered to make me more or less unsuitable for a stipendiary role. I was therefore advised to agree to enter the permanent non-stipendiary category of clergy. I have always worked in rural multi-parish benefices and have been Diocesan Adviser to the Bishop in the role of Dean of NSM/MSE for around three years, building on a background in adult education.

My experience of SSM

Here in Worcester we put together a booklet describing some of the things our SSMs do. Its title ('You Do *What*?') says it all. We've a long way to go in terms of recognition and understanding. For me, combining work and ministry is a fundamental expression of who I am. I think the majority of non-stipendiary clergy are both SSMs and MSEs. I have tried to consider some form of stipendiary ministry but sometimes the system isn't terribly flexible as far as SSMs are concerned and it is difficult to begin a sensible conversation.

What's the main focus of my ministry?

When I started in ministry I was managing director of our family marketing company; later I ran a B&B, and now I am a partner in our family specialist nursery business. My day job is running our online retail water plant business. It's a full-time job, focused on growing and advising customers about plants and also handling online orders. I work four days a week.

I have always believed that our ministry should be outward-facing. I have worked in several benefices located between 10 and 40 minutes from home. Latterly, I have tried as much as possible to promote SSM's presence within the committee structure of the diocese, so am deanery rep on Diocesan Synod and Diocesan Board of Social Responsibility.

Support and training

I trained on the West of England Ministerial Training Course. On the whole this was a good experience but sometimes it felt as if we were very isolated from the diocesan hierarchy. My curacy was not easy – I had to cover both a sabbatical and a vacancy and at one point was the only priest in the benefice. That felt very isolating and I don't think the Church currently does enough to prepare SSMs for the very real possibility that they may have to run the whole show at very little notice. Then what often follows is that SSMs are largely sidelined and ignored during the appointment of a new incumbent.

Challenges and difficulties

For me, the hardest part of SSM has been occasionally coming up against diocesan structures where SSMs are not understood or valued. Although, for a variety of reasons, I have chosen to move from benefice to benefice, local congregations have always been very understanding and supportive of my SSM role. The greater struggle is to help people in authority to recognize the very real strengths in what SSMs offer. In many ways the pressures of the role are very real and in general I feel that there is very little recognition by diocesan staff of the support we sometimes need in order to spin the plates we need to spin.

The best thing about SSM

The space and time that SSM has provided has allowed me to undertake a range of teaching roles, working with students progressing towards being awarded the Bishop's Certificate. I've always enjoyed cascading ideas and supporting people who want to become more involved in church and I have been privileged to share the students' journey with many people exploring what ministry might mean for them.

I enjoy baptisms, weddings and funerals because I love working with people beyond the radar of the local church. SSMs, who are grounded in the 'real' world, often seem to have a more generous attitude towards people on the periphery and more of an idea about what they are seeking and able to accept from those within the Church than diocesan staff.

Looking forward

Due to a change in circumstances, I am soon to retire from ministry, but am still concerned about what the next generation of clergy will be dealing with. I wonder also if the Church as a whole is aware of the tremendous cost savings provided by SSMs. It's worrying that some MSEs get virtually no recognition or support. We undervalue the fact that all SSMs employed outside the Church are *both* MSEs *and* ministers in a church context, and often the Church only 'clocks' the value of that part of our time which is given to working in the parish.

12

Discussion guidelines –
SSMs and MSEs

The aim of this chapter is to encourage useful conversations. This includes conversations between selectors and SSM candidates, between SSM curates and those supervising them, and between serving SSMs and colleagues responsible for their review and development.

Senior clergy hear complaints about their lack of support to certain groups. In fairness, a great deal of excellent work is done for all ministers, often on a shoestring. Most professionals responsible for clergy training and development readily agree that more could be done for SSMs and a lot more for MSEs. With declining budgets, such support will need to be high on imagination and low on delivery cost.

There are some things that might be considered as fundamental and not resource-heavy. One recommendation takes priority. Anyone selecting potential SSMs and MSEs, supporting them in pre- and post-ordination training and planning for clergy deployment and development, might begin with a single question: '*What is the main focus of your ministry?*'

This is the vital, often unasked question. It is a question that needs to be asked during selection, during training and brought into every review. It helps provide clarity about calling and what a minister is *for*. This is a focus that can change, but it needs to be identified and the implications thought about. Asking the question does not assume that candidates for SSM can custom-design their future, but hopefully they will begin to see decisions they can make about gaining skills, experience and starting to manage their own personal development. Exploring this question in depth helps to shape plans for training and will later lead to more realistic working agreements – useful and relevant to both the individual minister and the communities who will be served. There will inevitably be compromises – but at least they will be documented and clear.

There are three likely answers to this question about the focus of ministry.

1   Where the **parish** is clearly going to be the main focus, discussions still need to take place about time commitment, especially if the SSM is in work or has other significant commitments.
2   Sometimes candidates feel their focus of ministry will be divided between **work and parish**. This requires that attention be paid to meeting demands in both areas and making sure that workplace ministry is not sidelined.
3   If, however, an individual's main focus is **work**, time needs to be found to enable that calling – while at the same time being realistic about the Church's expectations about learning outcomes and future ministry. Discussion needs to reflect on how this ministry will be effective, recognized and supported. There can be no assumption that parochial contributions are to be ignored; MSEs need to be very clear about the fact that they will need to find time for parish experience and, after their curacy, they will probably be licensed to a parish.

Where an ordinand clearly has a calling to MSE, this needs to be worked out carefully. Much of the candidate's training will still, necessarily, be about parish ministry. However (and this would move us into new territory), opportunities could also be provided for learning, mentoring and interaction with other MSEs. Appropriate evidence from external-facing ministry should be accepted towards assessed training outcomes. At the same time, MSEs (and SSMs with a strong focus outside the parish) must continue to understand they are expected to acquire skills relating to future parish responsibilities.

As SSMs' roles develop, opportunities for discussion and reflection will present themselves in terms of selection, training and continuing professional development. The following sets out a range of principles, topics and discussion questions.

(Please note that the document 'SSM/MSE discussion guidelines' can be downloaded from <http://bit.ly/ssmdiscussion>.)

Vocations work

For those selecting potential SSMs

1   Candidates will benefit from discussions looking realistically at the demands of training and ministry for those who will continue in paid employment.
2   Early discussions about focus of ministry will help place candidates on a spectrum between parish-focused and work-focused activity.
3   Where a candidate's focus of ministry is likely to be substantially outside the parish, discussions about what kind of workplace or community ministry is envisaged will be helpful to understand the shape of their calling.
4   Even at this stage it's worth exploring associate leadership skills, exploring how far individuals see themselves as influencers of change.

For those selecting potential MSEs

1   MSE remains an important form of ordained ministry and currently needs more recognition and exploration. Those selecting candidates need to be familiar with this form of ministry and more attuned to its value and impact.
2   Urgent attention needs to be given to the assumption that MSEs can only be accepted for ministry if they have a written employer agreement. This does not reflect current work cultures and forces potential MSEs to present inappropriately as 'conventional' SSMs.
3   Where the candidate's primary focus of ministry is the workplace, discussions should actively explore evidence of the candidate's current workplace ministry. Explorations should focus on how ordination might enhance this.
4   Candidates should also be invited to understand how MSE is necessarily constrained by the Church's parish-focused training requirements.

5   Selection criteria might be adapted (or interpreted more flexibly) to seek out and recognize evidence acquired from work, including associate leadership skills.

Ordination training (IME phase 1)

For those directing and supporting SSMs in ordination training

1   SSMs in training should have the opportunity to study something of the history and scope of SSM.
2   They should have opportunities to reflect theologically on SSM.
3   They should be encouraged to understand and reflect on the pressures they will experience undertaking future ministry while also fulfilling other commitments, including work and family.
4   Opportunities should be given to develop the collaborative skills required in associate ministry.
5   Opportunities should be provided to meet and hear from other SSMs during training.

For those directing and supporting MSEs in ordination training

1   Ideally, all ministerial training should touch on workplace ministry, both lay and ordained, as valid aspects of mission and evangelism.
2   MSEs in training should be encouraged to understand and reflect on the pressures they will experience attempting to minister in both work and church.
3   Opportunities should be provided for studying the history of MSE (and workplace ministry in general) and to reflect theologically on this ministry.
4   Opportunities should be provided to meet and hear from other MSEs during training.
5   An effective MSE will expect to have the opportunity to undertake training in workplace ministry and to observe this form of ministry in action.

Curates in training (IME phase 2)

For those directing and supporting SSMs in post-ordination training

1 It is helpful to identify training incumbents with some experience of working with SSMs. If this is not possible, it is useful to have an experienced SSM as a mentor.
2 SSM curates need to reflect carefully on how they can fulfil learning agreements while managing other commitments. Curates need to remember to incorporate preparation time in their plans, plus time for study and attending learning events.
3 Ministry outside the parochial context (where appropriate) should be recognized and recorded as part of training agreements and evidence from it presented to fulfil assessment criteria.
4 Competences assessed should include those being exercised in other contexts.

For those directing and supporting MSEs in post-ordination training

1 More flexibility and realism can be applied in terms of licensing new MSEs. Those ordaining MSEs should not expect written employer agreements, but should still find opportunities to recognize the MSE's future contribution to a sector of work (for example, an ordinand might be 'licensed to the parish of St Elsewhere and also as MSE focused on the insurance industry').
2 It is helpful to identify training incumbents who have experience of working with MSEs or at least with SSMs. If this is not possible, it is useful to have an experienced MSE (or SSM in full-time work) as a mentor.
3 Learning agreements should continue to be realistic about how many hours can be committed to a curacy. Detailed consideration should be given to how the MSE will be trained in key aspects of parish ministry. Agreements should begin by determining the main focus of ministry, leading to a training plan that is realistic in encompassing both the learning outcomes required by the Church and the developmental needs of the SSM.

4 Workplace ministry should be recognized and developed within learning agreements and appropriate evidence from it presented to fulfil assessment criteria. Competences assessed should include those exercised in the workplace – for example, collaborative and team working and communication skills.

Long-term ministerial development

For those training, developing and supporting SSMs

1 Diocesan staff tasked with clergy development need to be familiar with the ministry experiences of SSMs at different stages of development. Particular attention needs to be given to longer-term development opportunities.
2 Template working agreements should be made available to demonstrate best practice. These should acknowledge ministry outside the parochial context.
3 Continuing attention needs to be given to the work–life balance of SSMs and any changes in their focus of ministry.
4 Ministry development review (MDR) processes can be more closely adapted to the needs of SSMs. Where MDR only gathers evidence relating to parish activity, this ignores huge areas of experience.
5 Where possible, reviewers should be SSMs or experienced in working closely with SSMs.
6 SSMs benefit from and appreciate tailored support and learning events. These need to be timed on a flexible basis to match the needs of the local SSM community.

For those training, developing and supporting MSEs

1 MDR processes can be more closely adapted to the needs of MSEs. At present MDR tends not to gather information about workplace engagement.
2 Diocesan staff tasked with clergy development need to be familiar with the work of MSEs and their stages of development.
3 Training and support should be provided for the tasks of workplace ministry.

4   Template working agreements should be made available to demonstrate best practice. These should acknowledge and record the MSE's work.
5   MSEs often feel ignored because it is assumed they do not achieve measurable outcomes in terms of church growth. Other equally relevant criteria relating to outreach should be applied.
6   Opportunities for theological reflection should be provided so that MSEs can build on their workplace experience and relate it to the life of the Church.
7   MSEs benefit from tailored support and learning events and the chance to interact with other MSEs. Numbers within any one diocese may make this impracticable – regional events often make sense.

Questions for ministry development reviews (MDR)

Suggested questions are set out below for those conducting MDR conversations, who will no doubt expand on this basic list. These example questions may also help SSMs and MSEs prepare for review discussions (italicized text in brackets provides additional notes for reviewees).

Review questions for SSMs and MSEs

1   What is the main focus of your ministry? What makes you clear/unclear about that?
2   How far has this focus changed since ordination?
3   What difference does ordination make to that ministry?
4   How close is SSM/MSE to what you expected?
5   What is your main role and contribution within the church community where you are licensed?
6   How far does your working agreement reflect your current situation?
7   Tell me about your ministry outside church? (*It's good to have opportunities to talk about what you do rather than just what the Church wants to hear about.*)
8   Where do you make your biggest contribution as an SSM/MSE?
9   How could your ministry be more effective?
10 How could your ministry be more supported?

11 How have you been stretched in your ministry?

12 Where have you been surprised by your ability to overcome difficulties or take on new challenges?

13 How has your ministry developed in the last 12 months?

14 Where have you taken on additional responsibility?

15 How far do you exercise associate leadership?

16 What opportunities have you identified to broaden your ministry and gain new experience?

17 How do you plan to extend your skills and knowledge in the future?

18 How far are you aware about how SSM/MSE happens elsewhere? Who can you talk to, so you can find out?

19 Who will you turn to for support? (*It helps to find a mentor or spiritual director with experience of, or at least sympathy for, SSM/ MSE as a distinctive form of ministry.*)

20 How can you meet other SSMs/MSEs?

21 Where can you find inspiration? Where can you find models of good practice?

22 Where can you find tools to assist you to think theologically about SSM/MSE?

23 What about parish ministry? What is your contribution to the diocese? (*Be prepared for the fact that, as well as evidence outlined above, you will need to show how you've contributed to the context where you are licensed.*)

Review questions mainly for MSEs

1 Where do you make your biggest contribution as an MSE? How clear are you about the nature of the workplace ministry you undertake?

2 How far is your ministry noticed and recognized?

3 How far do you feel your work colleagues understand your role as an MSE?

4 How are you going to identify or negotiate appropriate opportunities for learning? (*You may not be taught about the work of MSEs as part of any formal training programme, but that does not mean that you cannot negotiate opportunities to include study in this area.*)

5   In training programmes, what explorations can you make about ways in which your workplace ministry might be recognized and, where possible, assessed in order to meet learning outcomes?

6   Longer term, are you continuing to learn about workplace ministry? How far are you aware of (or seeking to identify) opportunities for continuing professional development as a workplace minister?

7   How do you manage the parts of your role not focused on the workplace? (*You will be required to undertake activities and gain experience that may seem irrelevant to workplace ministry. You need to give proper time and attention to these tasks. Careful negotiation will sometimes reveal how this can be done while working full time or at least point to those areas where you need to compromise.*)

8   How much reflection have you undertaken about your specific workplace ministry? What evidence from this can you present to the Church? What examples do you have, for example, of workplace pastoral encounters, evangelism or prophetic ministry?

Appendix: SSM/MSE
working agreement template

(See Chapter 9 for more details about working agreements. Please note that the document 'SSM/MSE working agreement template' can be downloaded from <http://bit.ly/ssmagreement>.)

WORKING AGREEMENT FOR A SELF-SUPPORTING MINISTER, DIOCESE OF _____

NOTES – to be read before drafting a working agreement.

This document serves as an example of a working agreement for ordained clergy serving as self-supporting ministers (SSMs) within the Diocese of _____. This includes ministers in secular employment (MSEs).

This document is not a contract, nor is it an inflexible template. It is designed to enable positive and productive discussions between the SSM and incumbent. Nevertheless, it needs to be realistic and to contain as much useful detail as possible.

During discussion it may be helpful to refer to the standard Clergy Terms of Service published at _____.

Working agreements can easily become out of date, like any job description. They can be overambitious, constraining or have very little relationship to reality. They can accurately describe a working relationship or carefully avoid dealing with difficult issues. They can outline unrealistic expectations, on either side. They can also be extremely helpful in checking assumptions and anticipating areas of tension or role conflict.

The wording used is less important than the relationship the document describes. Where there is trust, good communication and open feedback, a written agreement will simply document what is already working. A working agreement cannot guarantee that things will work well, but an out-of-date or inaccurate agreement often leads to problems.

The most important aspect of any working agreement is the conversations that take place around it. Before the agreement is drawn up the SSM and incumbent should have a detailed and frank discussion exploring: mutual and separate expectations of both individuals; the skills and experience of the SSM (particularly those gained in secular employment); the skills and experience of the incumbent and other team members; the expectations and needs of the SSM's family; the expectations, plans and needs of the worshipping community; the time the SSM has to offer and how that might vary during a typical year.

It is helpful for the SSM and incumbent to be open with each other about their relative strengths and weaknesses and understand each other's previous experience, so that the complementary nature of their ministry is recognized and affirmed. Such a discussion may usefully identify any areas of theological/liturgical difference. It is essential, of course, that appropriate confidentiality is kept and mutual public support and respect are exercised in treating all matters under discussion.

When the working agreement is being designed, detailed consideration should be given to the way it will be reviewed. For a new post-holder it is usually important to undertake an initial review after six months.

The post-holder and incumbent will each keep a copy of the agreed document. It is often useful for churchwardens also to have a copy. During a vacancy it will generally be appropriate for a rural/area dean to receive a copy.

WORKING AGREEMENT

Name of minister:	Parish/benefice:
Agreement date:	Date of next review of this document:

1 Context for ministry

Revd **Name** (*use full name here and then first name elsewhere in this document*) serves as Associate Priest (SSM) (*insert alternative role title as appropriate*), first licensed to _____ parish/benefice on *date*.

Name's principal role is one of support and general assistance to Revd **Name** (*incumbent: use full name here and then first name elsewhere in this document*), (*insert role title of incumbent*).

2 Contact

Name can be contacted regarding parish/benefice matters on *telephone number*.

3 Focus of ministry

A description of the SSM's main focus of ministry. In a parish context? In the community? At work? Where the SSM also operates as a Minister in Secular Employment (add details and supplementary documents as required) this will probably need a separate paragraph at this point in the working agreement.

4 Broader context

Description of the SSM's secular work and other commitments.

Name and *incumbent Name* will attempt to be flexible around both parish/benefice commitments and *Name*'s work commitments (*refer to working hours here if the SSM has an external job*).

5 Wider church responsibilities held by the SSM

List any church roles and responsibilities held outside the parish/ benefice, e.g. diocesan roles or work undertaken for national organizations.

6 Special responsibilities within the parish/benefice

Name will have particular responsibility for _____ (*specify any particular responsibilities, e.g. mission/ministry planning, organization of study groups, administrative tasks, schools work, involvement in the local community, etc.*).

7 Time commitment within the parish/benefice

The SSM's time spent on parochial duties will include time for leading worship, taking occasional offices (including preparation and follow-up), meetings, reading, prayer and sermon preparation. Time spent within the parish/benefice needs to take account of special responsibilities, wider church responsibilities and the SSM's commitments outside the faith community – see above.

Name will offer, on average:

a) *XX* hours per week to the parish/benefice.
b) *XX* Sundays per month where he/she will be leading worship.
c) *Name* will preach approximately *XX* times a month at Sunday services, plus addresses and homilies where required.
d) Approximately *XX* additional services each month (including midweek services).
e) Approximately *XX* funerals per year, *XX* weddings per year, plus *XX* baptisms per year. (*It is generally useful to specify how far the SSM will be involved in receiving bookings and handling paperwork for occasional offices.*)
f) Refer to additional expectations e.g. daily offices.

8 Time off

Name's day off is _____. *Name* will take *XX* weeks' holiday a year from his/her paid employment and will give as much notice as possible to fit in with parish/benefice rotas. *Name* and *incumbent Name* will work as closely as possible to coordinate holiday dates.

9 Meetings with the incumbent

Name and *incumbent Name* will meet:

a) *XX* times a month to deal with administrative matters.
b) *XX* times a month/quarter to provide mutual support, opportunities for personal review and growth, and theological reflection.

10 Ministry team and other meetings

As a licensed SSM priest (*amend as necessary*), *Name* is a full member of the PCC/all PCCs within the benefice (*amend as necessary*).

Name will attend meetings as follows:

a) *Name* will be expected to attend ministry team meetings and meetings of (*specify details*) where he/she is available.
b) *Name* will attend PCC, Deanery Chapter and Deanery Synod meetings *on an occasional basis/specify agreed attendance.*
c) OR: In general terms, *Name* proposes to attend parish/benefice meetings where his/her attendance is particularly relevant rather than attending on a routine, ex officio basis.

11 Pastoral work

Although *Name* has limited availability for pastoral work and visits, he/she recognizes that specific pastoral need or staffing availability will on occasions require him/her to undertake work of this nature (*specify details as appropriate, including details of home communions*). Since such work can often be time-consuming, this will be subject to regular review.

12 Confidentiality

Name will indicate to congregation members that, unless express agreement is made to the contrary, all matters disclosed to him/her during the course of his/her duties may be disclosed to *incumbent Name.*

13 Office space/secretarial support/resources

Name will have access to (*specify office space, secretarial support, etc.*).

14 Clerical dress – everyday and liturgical

Normal liturgical dress for eucharistic services is alb and stole/cassock and surplice (*specify details*). *Name* will wear a clerical collar at all times when leading worship and (*as agreed*).

15 Representing the parish/benefice/incumbent

Name understands that there may be instances where he/she is asked to represent or stand in for *incumbent Name* at meetings (*specify details as necessary*).

16 Expenses

Name will claim travel expenses monthly/quarterly from (*agreed contact*) who has responsibility for the parish/benefice finances. Relevant car travel will be reimbursed at the current diocesan rate per mile. (*Provide details of other expenses that might be claimed, e.g. books for study. Provide details of when and how PCCs will be made aware of expenses and how these are essential costs in SSM.*)

17 Payment of fees

As a Self-Supporting Minister, *Name* understands that his/her ministry is unpaid. *Name* notes that in _____ Diocese, SSMs are not entitled to receive fees for services, including occasional offices, and that this remains the case during a vacancy (*or, set out alternative diocesan policy on payment of SSMs for occasional offices*).

18 Time for ministerial formation/continuing professional development

Name recognizes his/her need to take responsibility to seek opportunities for continuing professional development, supported by *incumbent Name* and the local faith community. Plans for the next 12 months will include (*provide details here, possibly based on a recent MDR; these plans need to be realistic in terms of time and will sometimes mean that other duties have to be put aside temporarily*).

He/she plans to allocate *XX* days per quarter/year for learning events, ministerial formation and/or study. He/she plans to make a private retreat at least once a year.

19 Ministerial support

Specify what arrangements are in place for the SSM in terms of mentoring, coaching and other forms of professional support. It may be helpful to note that the SSM has a spiritual director or some similar supporter, although it is inappropriate to specify further details in a Working Agreement.

20 Grievance procedure

Name and *incumbent Name* agree that any misunderstandings and/or grievances they experience will be discussed in private; never in public. We note in principle that *Name* should be free to contribute openly and with integrity to discussions within the parish but should also demonstrate loyalty to colleagues and church officers. *Name* and *incumbent Name* therefore agree to support each other publicly but maintain their individual viewpoints and contributions. If any issue cannot be resolved and is too fundamental for colleagues simply to agree to differ, then advice should be sought from the Archdeacon or Suffragan Bishop.

21 Review of this document

It is suggested that a new working agreement should be reviewed after six months, then afterwards every 12 months or longer may be appropriate. The Agreement should be reviewed where there is any significant change in circumstances (such as changes in personnel, unpredicted work pressures, health issues).

The date this document will next be reviewed is indicated at the top of this document.

Signed:

Revd *Name of incumbent*	**Revd *Name of the SSM***
Role title	Role title

Notes

1 Are you a vicar or what?

1 <www.churchofengland.org/sites/default/files/2017-10/2012ministry-statistics.pdf>

2 A question of identity

1 <http://trushare.com/46MAR99/mr99nsms.htm>

3 A brief history

1 For a comprehensive history of unpaid ordained ministry, see the work of Patrick Vaughan (a digest appears in Fuller and Vaughan (1986), p. 117 onwards).

4 At the turning point?

1 'Is anybody listening?', *Anvil*, 14 April 1997.
2 <www.cpas.org.uk/download/1203/web_upload%252F8%2BOLM-supplement%2BRS09-single-1268750830.pdf>
3 <www.with-intent.confiteor.org.uk/the-theology.html>

6 Some theological resonances

1 For a thorough overview of the current range of ministry options, see Torry (2006).
2 <http://rowanwilliams.archbishopofcanterbury.org/articles.php/2097/the-christian-priest-today-lecture-on-the-occasion-of-the-150th-an-niversary-of-ripon-college-cuddesd>
3 Steven Croft, May 2013, <https://blogs.oxford.anglican.org/tag/ministry-division/>.
4 Alister McGrath, 'The future looks nothing like the godless and reli-gionless world so confidently predicted 40 years ago', *Christianity Today*, March 2005 ('The twilight of atheism').
5 *Common Worship: Services and Prayers for the Church of England* (2000) London: Church House Publishing, p. 411.
6 *Common Worship*, p. 291.
7 <www.aftersunday.org.uk>

9 Making it work

1 See also Nash, Pimlott and Nash (2008), for a range of practical tips on collaborative working.

2 See also Lawson (2000), for practical tips on working in an associate role, including suggestions for mutual mentoring.

10 Developing your ministry

1 <www.churchgrowthrd.org.uk/blog/sharedinsight/interim_ministry_key_learning_points>

11 The future shape of SSM

1 *Church Times*, 7 February 2014.

2 <www.auckanglican.org.nz/what-we-do/local-shared-ministry>

3 See, for example, <www.gracenola.org/three-bi-vocational-pastors/> as well as books by Dennis Bickers.

4 'Shaping vicars: A "game of unreality"', April 2013, <www.freshexpressions.org.uk/views/shaping-vicars>.

5 *Church Times*, 7 February 2014.

References and further reading

Aisthorpe, Steve (2016) *The Invisible Church: Learning from the experiences of churchless Christians*. Edinburgh: Saint Andrew Press.

Allen, Roland (1923) *Voluntary Clergy*. London: SPCK.

Atwell, Robert (2013) *The Good Worship Guide: Leading liturgy well*. London: Canterbury Press.

Barry, Frank Russell (1935) *The Relevance of the Church*. London: Nisbet.

Bickers, Dennis (2004) *The Bivocational Pastor: Two jobs, one ministry*. Kansas City: Beacon Hill Press.

Bonhoeffer, Dietrich (2015) *Letters and Papers from Prison*. Minneapolis, MN: Fortress Press.

Borg, Marcus (1997) *The God We Never Knew*. San Francisco, CA: Harper.

Clinton, Mike (2014) 'A closer look at self-supporting and stipendiary ministers in the Experience of Ministry Survey 2013 dataset'. London: King's College.

Cocksworth, Christopher and Brown, Rosalind (2006) *Being a Priest Today: Exploring priestly identity*. Norwich: Canterbury Press.

Ecclestone, Alan, Sheldrake, Philip, Wakefield, Gordon and Walker, Michael (1986) *Spirituality and Human Wholeness*. London: Churches Together in Britain and Ireland.

Edwards, David (1961) *Priests and Workers*. London: SCM Press.

Fox, Matthew (1995) *The Reinvention of Work*. San Francisco, CA: Harper Collins.

Francis, James and Francis, Leslie J (1998) *Tentmaking: Perspectives on self-supporting ministry*. Leominster: Gracewing.

Fuller, John and Vaughan, Patrick (1986) *Working for the Kingdom: The story of ministers in secular employment*. London: SPCK.

Greenwood, Robin (1994) *Transforming Priesthood*. London: SPCK.

Hacking, Rod (1990) *On the Boundary: A vision for nonstipendiary ministry*. Norwich: Canterbury Press.

Hoskins, Jeffrey and Torry, Malcolm (2006) *Ordained Local Ministry: A theological exploration and practical handbook*. Norwich: Canterbury Press.

Hodge, Mark (1983) *Non-stipendiary Ministry in the Church of England*. London: General Synod.

Hoyle, David (2016) *The Pattern of Our Calling*. London: SCM Press.

Kuhrt, Gordon (2001) *Ministry Issues for the Church of England*. London: Church House Publishing.

Larive, Armand E. (2006) *After Sunday*. London: Continuum.

Lawson, Kevin E. (2000) *How to Thrive in Associate Staff Ministry.* Herndon, VA: Alban Institute.

Lewis-Anthony, Justin (2009) *If You Meet George Herbert on the Road, Kill Him: Radically re-thinking priestly ministry.* London: Mowbray.

Mantle, John (2000) *Britain's First Worker-priests.* London: SCM Press.

Moltmann, Jürgen (1992) *The Spirit of Life.* London: SCM Press.

Morgan, Teresa (2011) 'Self-supporting ministry in the Church of England and the Anglican churches of Wales, Scotland and Ireland: Report of the national survey 2010'. Oxford: Teresa Morgan.

Nash, Sally, Pimlott, Jo and Nash, Paul (2008) *Skills for Collaborative Ministry.* London: SPCK.

Percy, Martyn (2006) *Clergy: The origin of species.* London: Continuum.

Peyton, Nigel and Gatrell, Caroline (2013) *Managing Clergy Lives: Obedience, sacrifice, intimacy.* London: Bloomsbury.

Picardo, Rosario (2013) *Ministry Makeover: Recovering a theology for bi-vocational service in the Church.* Eugene, OR: Wipf and Stock.

Pink, Daniel H. (2011) *Drive: The surprising truth about what motivates us.* Edinburgh: Canongate.

Pritchard, John (2007) *The Life and Work of a Priest.* London: SPCK.

Ramsey, Michael (1972) *The Christian Priest Today.* London: SPCK.

Russell, Anthony (1980) *The Clerical Profession.* London: SPCK.

Smith, Magdalen (2014) *Steel Angels: The personal qualities of a priest.* London: SPCK.

Stevens, Anthony (2004) *The Roots of War and Terror.* London: Continuum.

Stevens, R. Paul (1985) *Liberating the Laity: Equipping all the saints for ministry.* London: IVP.

Torry, Malcom (2006) *Diverse Gifts: Varieties of ministry in the local church and community.* Norwich: Canterbury Press.

Vaughan, Patrick (1987) 'Non-stipendiary ministry in the Church of England: A history of the development of an idea', PhD thesis, University of Nottingham. Available online at: <http://eprints.nottingham.ac.uk/11248/1/380134.pdf>.

Ward, Jenna and McMurray, Robert (2016) *The Dark Side of Emotional Labour.* London: Routledge.

Witcombe, John (ed.) (2012) *The Curate's Guide: From calling to first parish.* London: Church House Publishing.

Other publications

Archbishops' Council (2017) 'Setting God's people free'. London: Church of England Renewal and Reform.

Church in Wales (2012) 'Church in Wales review'. Cardiff: Church in Wales.

Church in Wales (2014) 'The governing body of the Church in Wales: Ministry report'. Cardiff: Church in Wales.

Church of England Ministry Division (2017) 'Calling far and wide project: Assistant ministers, summary report'. London: Church of England Ministry Division.

Church of England Research and Statistics (2016) 'Ministry statistics in focus: Stipendiary clergy projections 2015–2035'. London: Church of England Research and Statistics.

Diocese of Auckland (2016) *Local Shared Ministry Handbook*. Auckland: Diocese of Auckland.

Diocese of Exeter (2003) 'Moving on in mission and ministry: The final report of the working party exploring future patterns of ministry'. Exeter: Diocese of Exeter.

Press and Publications Board of the Church Assembly (1945) *Towards the Conversion of England*. London: Press and Publications Board of the Church Assembly.

Scottish Episcopal Church (2011) *Whole Church Mission and Ministry Policy*. Mission and Ministry Board.